TECHNIQUES OF END-GAME IN CHESS

TECHNIQUES OF END-GAME IN CHESS

B. K. CHATURVEDI

GOODWILL PUBLISHING HOUSE®
B-3 RATTAN JYOTI, 18 RAJENDRA PLACE
NEW DELHI -110008 (INDIA)

Published by
GOODWILL PUBLISHING HOUSE®
B-3 Rattan Jyoti, 18 Rajendra Place
New Delhi-110008 (INDIA)
Tel. : 25750801, 25820556
Fax : 91-11-25764396
E-mail : goodwillpub@vsnl.net
website : www.goodwillpublishinghouse.com

Printed at :-
Kumar Offset Printers
New Delhi

CONTENTS

Preface

The present work is the third book in the series of books on this royal game. Despite being the important link of the series each of these books is complete in itself. That is why a few chapters on the basics and the laws have been deliberately repeated. The idea is not to deprive the reader of only one book of the niceties of the whole game. The whole intention is to make these books useful for all the categories of the chess-lovers: those who are initiated and those who are not shall also find these books suiting to their requirements.

Like the human body cannot be compart-mentalised for treatment because it contains just one life and not the series of the bits of life to constitute one whole life, so is true with this most brainy game: Chess! When one goes to play one doesn't play only in stages. But as they have segregated the human organs for the convenience of study, likewise these books have been devised for the sake of their better comprehension by their discerning readers.

Furthermore, like the eyes are believed to be the most expressive organs of the human body, so is this last phase of the chess play, known as the end-game. It is in here that the dazzling display of one's mastery over the moves and positions manifests in its best form; it is that link of the whole that decides the entire fate of the whole. Since this stage is akin to last ditch battle, more deeds are required than the words of promise in this stage. Hence the plethora of more than three hundred diagrams to drive home the point. All these charts have been culled from the variety of books on the subject and the seen games for which the author is deeply grateful. It is impossible to thank all of them for they include from the mediocres to the masters and from the bizzare to the brilliant. It is earnestly hoped that these books will contribute their mite in seeing the blossoming of a few more Vishwanathan Anand.

Lastly the author expresses his deep gratitude to Mr. S. K. Chaturvedi and S. C. Chaturvedi whose deep knowledge in the game came very handy to him. And the author has no words to express all that he feels about Mr. Anand Sagar Chowdhry of 'Goodwill Publications' who has not only been the 'all-problem solver' but the very soul of this present series. May the tribe increase!

—B. K. CHATURVEDI

"CHESS IS AN ART; CHESS IS A STUDY; CHESS IS ONE OF THE NOBLEST INVENTION OF THE HUMAN MIND"

—C. E. M. Joad

I

THE END-GAME PLAY

Although the name suggests it to be the dessert of the chess-feast, in reality it is not only the end course but the whole meal, for, this stage decides who among the players is going to pay the bill for the feast! It is in this stage that the dazzling moves, the master-moves are manifest in their full cry. Now, at this stage the board has much less material and the moves are almost fixed. A player's true strength and ability can be judged reliably from this final phase of the struggle. It might be just the link to the whole but it is that link that determines the whole fate of the whole! Nothing lies hidden or held in store in this last ditch battle-phase wherein even the crown has to move like the pieces to defend his forces and attack. The concluding stage of a game of chess has its characteristic peculiarities, which, in comparison with the middle game, alter the whole approach to the positions and the significance of the forces in action on the board.

This is the stage when you think to gaining maximum use of your pieces. For success it is important to know how to get maximum activity out of the pieces and to organise the cooperation of the pieces among themselves and with the pawns. To play the end-game correctly means to make one's fighting forces active to the greatest possible extent and to assure their smooth cooperation. In this stage you can't keep the pieces unused to consolidate your position. No more Rooks guarding the fort or the Kings castled in safety. It is an all out war, the final battle. Each piece has got to be active and mobile.

It is due to the heavy demands made by this phase on your ability, alertness and the far-reaching vision that the beginners often tend to commit mistakes. But remember a mistake committed in this phase is tantamount to commuting at least ten in the other phases of the game. For, in other phases, you might get a chance of redeeming them. But in this stage even a minor mistake might cost you the game. You have to be doubly sure of what you are doing. Even if you allow the opponent's a mere Pawn to escape, it might boomerang upon you in the form of the promoted Queen.

In the end game it is rarely possible even with the big material advantage to mate the opponent's King at once, rendering all your precious advantages, mobility, tempi gained in the earlier phase the useless nothings! You must generate more forces by endeavouring to promote your Pawns. This means that since every "insignificant" Pawn may, given a chance, return with the mighty force of the Queen or the bulldozing Rook, the roles of Pawn become greatly increased. That is why the Pawn play is of great significance in this part of the game. Pawn promotion is one of the strategically indispensable tasks of the end-game play.

In comparison to the opening stages or the middle game stage, it is relatively easier to study the end game with its small number of pieces and pawns. In the development of the chess theory over the years, scores of endgame positions have been thoroughly analysed and published in the literature of the game. In these positions, the best methods of attack and defence have been found and the final outcome, granted correct play on the both sides has been determined. Furthermore, for may endings typical playing procedures have been established and auxillary methods worked out which permit a rapid and accurate appreciation of the position. Ending which have been investigated like this are called theoretical. It is these endings that gave birth to the composition of the end-game problems which like the 'One Dayers' over the 'Test Matches' in cricket, are getting increasingly popular. There is hardly any newspaper or journal worth the name which doesn't come up with 'One-move Checkmate', 'Two Move Checkmate' problems on every Sunday for its avid readers and solvers.

This play, however, does not become theoretical immediately, though even the most complicated positions, typical manoeuvres, have now been elaborated and the best ways of playing discovered. Normally, the problem in a complex ending is to transpose it into the sort of positions that have already been studied. When learning chess one ought to begin with an analysis of simple positions with a small number of fighting units.

And these, as a rule, are the end-game positions. By analysing straight forward endings with the most varied combinations of material, the beginners can get to know the special characteristics of the various pieces and the mechanism of their struggle against each other. That is the reason why some selected end-game problems are also appended in the end of this book.

While discussing the end-game importance, we might have erroneously presumed all of our readers to have been initiated in the game. Some of you might not been initiated, though. Hence for their benefit we now give the 'basics' of the game; the properties of the Pieces, Pawns, the basic techniques, laws etc. In case you are initiated, neglect these details. But on the second thoughts, even for you, the initiated, it would be better to go through the following chapter in case you might have some confusion.

1.

Alice, now a promoted pawn, with the White Queen and the Red Queen.

Illustration by Tenniel to Lewis Carroll's Through the Looking-Glass and what Alice Found There.

II

BASICS OF CHESS

Chess has mightly been called the game of intellectuals because it calls for a keen and alert mind and concentration of the highest quality. Indeed it is the most serious game ever devised by man. Thus the basic requirements for being a good chess player are thorough knowledge of the game, sharp intellect and ability to concentration. These qualities, as is apparent, can be developed only by personal efforts and practice. The only aspects of playing chess which can be taught are the pattern of movement of the various pieces and the basic rules of the game. Then after it is for the individual player to master it and devise his own individual styles of play.

This game is played on a board having 16 pieces for each side to move them in the 64 squares available for their movement. Only two persons can play it. The details are the following:

(i) The Board

The chessboard is eight squares wide and eight squares long, thus a total area of 64 squares. In any row the light and dark squares alternate; in any diagonal the squares are ali of one colour. These colours of the squares on the board vary; they range from straight forward black and white to such off-beat combinations as green and blue or gold-flecked or silver-flecked. By convention, however, the lighter squares are called white and the darker ones black. And by convention, too, the board is placed between the players (who alternate in moving) so that each player has a white square in his lower right hand corner. The rows that point from one player to the other are called 'FILES'; the crossing rows are called 'RANKS'. The board is called 'Bisaat' in Urdu, Persian and 'Patti' in Hindi.

(ii) The Pieces

(a) **King:** The board is a battleground for 32 pieces; each side having: one King, one Queen, two Rooks, two Bishops, two Knights and eight Pawns. In colloquial parlance they are known as Badshah or Raja, Vazir or Rani, Pheela or Haathi, Oonta, Ghorha, and Paidal respectively. The most important piece—the one around which the whole game revolves—is the King. He is the largest piece and, in most traditionally designed sets, can be easily recognised by the cross he wears on his Crown. The figurative symbol for the king is ♔ for White and ♚ for Black; his abbreviation is K.

(b) **Queen:** The strongest piece on tne board is the Queen which has more authority and power than even the King which is just the prestige piece. In fact the Queen is the power behind the throne, and her status is indicated by her size. She is just a hair smaller than the King. Although deriving her authority from the King, the Queen is, in a practical sense more powerful than even the King. If the King is like the British King, the Queen is like the British Prime Minister. Unlike the King, however, she wears a Coronet, not a Crown and there is no cross to top her off. Her symbol is ♕ for White and ♛ for Black: her abbreviation is Q.

(c) **The Rook:** After the Queen it is the Rook that is most powerful. This piece looks like the tower of a castle. Many call it also the castle. This term 'Rook' is derived from the Persian word 'rouk' which means an elephant. In the exotic sets the Rook is, in fact as well as in name, an elephant, often carrying a howdah on its back. In standard sets which are called the Staunton Pattern after the English chess master, the piece looks like the symbol ♖ for White and ♜ for Black; and its abbreviation is R.

(d) **The Bishop :** This piece is identified with the slit in its head, which supposedly represents a Bishop's mitre, although it might also represent a court jester's hat as the French call this piece le Fou or the fool or the jester. Its symbol is ♗ for White and ♝ for Black and its abbreviation in notation is B.

(e) **The Knight:** This is the most fascination piece on the board. It has not changed its appearance since chess was invented. It is true that in many old, exotic and oriental sets it has a knight on horseback. Later on the knight disappeared but the horse remained. Hence its Hindi name Ghorha or the Horse. It is generally called Knight and represented by the symbol N in modern notations. Earlier it was also written as Kt. But the symbol got changed to N because the symbol 'Kt' confused it with the symbol 'K' for the King. It is only for its precise identification that it is written as N. Its figurative symbol is unmistakable ♘ for White and ♞ for Black.

(f) **The Pawn:** Now we come to the last piece, the Pawn. In all sets, no matter what their origin, no matter how radical their design, the Pawn is the smallest piece on the board. As though to make up for stature, there are more of them (8) than any other variety of pieces on the board. The Pawn is at the bottom of the power ladder but he cannot and often does not hold the big guns at bay. And often he can play the decisive role in a game. The symbol for White Pawn is ♙ and for Black Pawn is ♟. The abbreviation is P.

(iii) Setting the Board

The board is usually placed in such a way that each player has the last white square on the right-hand corner and the black square on the left-hand corner. The pieces in the board are put in the identical fashion. Let us begin with placing the White pieces.

Put one White Rook on the lower right-hand square and the other White Rook in the dark square at the lower left. Now, on the same rank (horizontal row), place a Knight next to Rook, then a Bishop next to each Knight. Now only the centre squares of the bottom rank should now be unoccupied. These are for the King and the Queen. The Queen always stands, at the start of the game, on a square of her own colour. Thus the White Queen should be placed on the left-hand centre square. The King stands next to her.

Now the principal pieces have been placed. The Pawns are next placed. Set them on the rank immediately in front of the principal pieces; one Pawn in front of every principal piece. This completes the starting line-up for White.

The same way place the Black pieces on the other side of the board. They are arranged precisely the way the White pieces are—Rooks occupying end squares, Knights next and then Bishops. Notice, however, that since the Queen always starts life on a square of her own colour she will, from Black's point of view, stand on the right-hand centre square.

What is important is to see whether the Queens are occupying the squares of their own colour respectively. This way the King faces King and the Queen faces Queen across the board.

Now your board should appear like this:

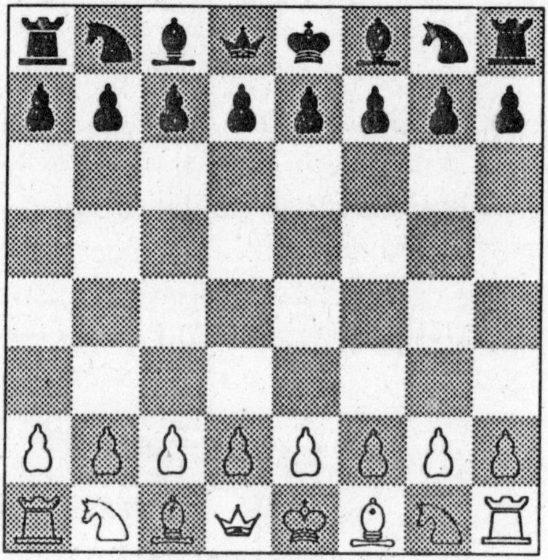

2

Traditionally in the charts White is deemed to be on the bottom side of the board and the Black on the top.

(iv) The Movement of the Pieces and their Manner of Capture (killing) of the Enemy Pieces

(a) **The Rook :** Study the diagram below. This is the position when you have cleared your board of all pieces and placed White Rook in the position as shown. The Rook moves in straight lines, along the ranks and files, as indicated by the arrows in the diagram.

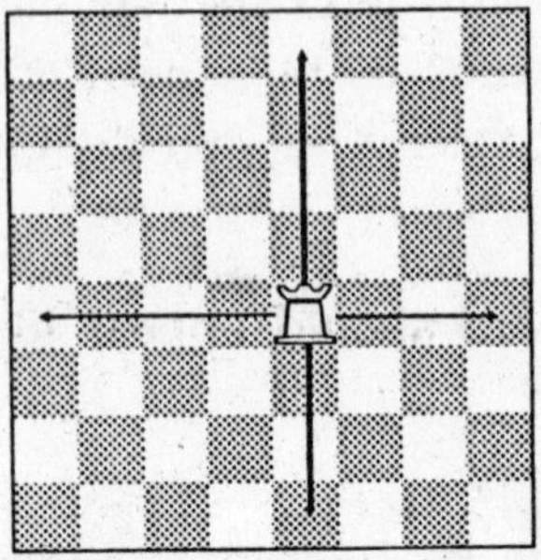

3

As long as the Rook's path is unobstructed there is nothing to stop him except the edge of the board. Any enemy piece within this range can be captured. The piece that is captured is removed from the board and the capturing piece takes its place. To illustrate the Rook's powers of capturing and attacking, let's add some pieces to the board.

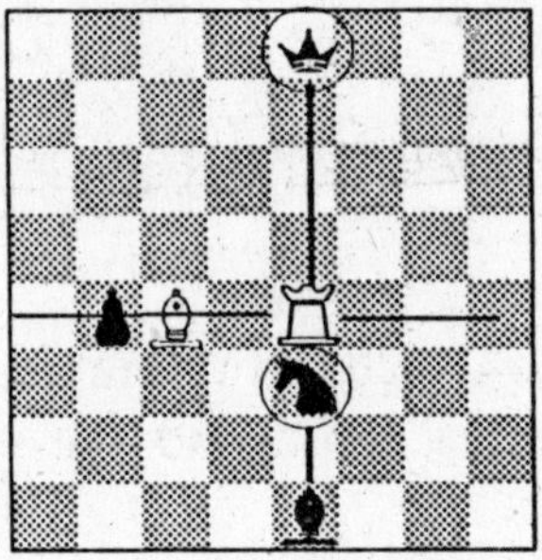

4

Now the Rook can capture the Black Queen who is with in his range on a file. The Black Pawn lies along the Rook's rank, but it cannot be captured because the White Bishop blocks the way. The Rook can't jump over any piece, his own or the enemy's. Thus, the Black Bishop is safe. But the Black Knight may be captured depending upon the sweet will of the player. Capture is not necessary.

In case the Rook were to capture the Queen, the board would look like this:

5

Notice the Black Queen disappearing from the board and the White Rook's capturing her place.

Now, to assess the powers of the Rook, clear your board again and put a Rook down on any square. Count the number of squares swept by the Rook's line of fire along the rank and file. Not counting the square on which he stands, the Rook commands 14 squares. Whatever place he stands, he will continue to threaten all the 14 squares provided there is no obstruction in his line of fire. This is one of the Rook's great powers; he always commands 14 squares no matter where he stands. Of course, if he is blocked by his own men his great range of fire becomes innocuous. And this is his biggest weakness; he can be all-too easily hemmed in by his own allies. He needs open lines along which he can exert his strength.

(b) The Bishop: Now place a White Bishop on a board bereft of all other pieces. The Bishop move the following way:

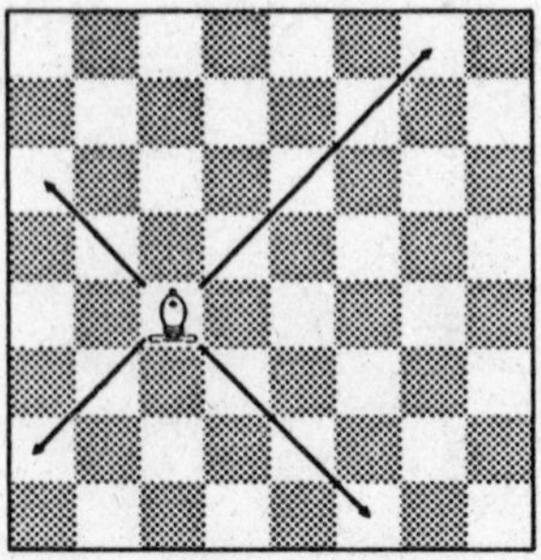

6

As you can see, the Bishop moves along diagonals and is confined to squares of one colour. It can command as many as 13 squares, but few as 7 (try putting the Bishop where the lower left-hand arrow-head is in the diagram; you will see that the Bishop's range has been cut down to 7 squares). Like the Rook it can capture any enemy piece that stands in its line of fire. And, like the Rook, it cannot jump over any pieces.

Let's add a few pieces on to the board to see how the Bishop captures:

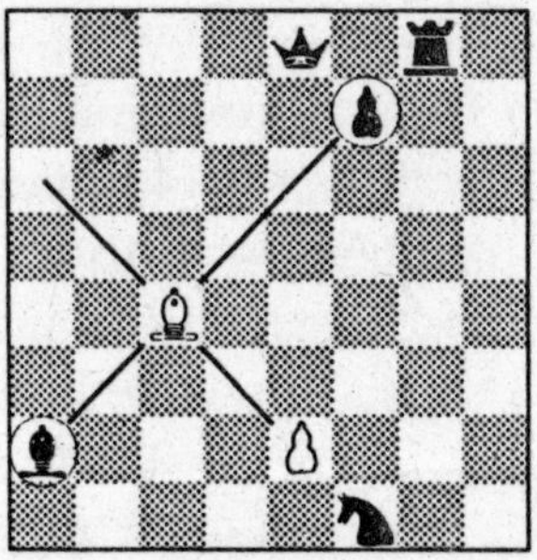

7

Two Black pieces can be captured—the Bishop and the Pawn. The Rook is safe because the Black Pawn blocks him from the Bishop's line of fire; the Knight is immune because one of the Bishop's own Pawn obstructs its line of fire. Also the Black Queen is out of the Bishop's range.

Now let's see what the board would look like if a capture were made. The White Bishop captures the Black Bishop. The board then looks like this:

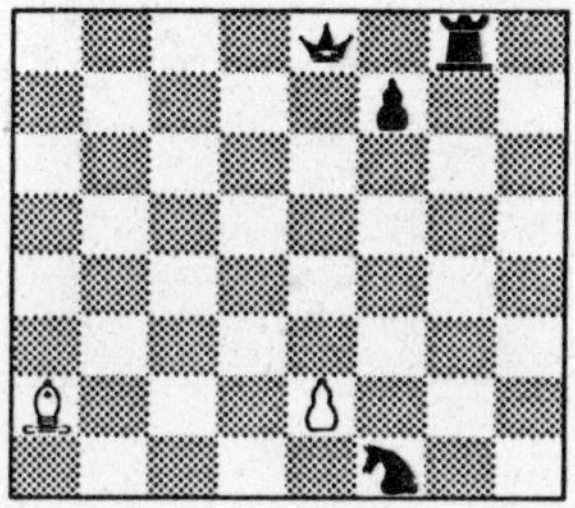

8

Notice the Black Bishop now gone and the White Bishop taking its place. Now see that the Bishop is still in a position to capture the Black Pawn.

(c) **The Queen:** As already explained this is the most powerful piece on the board. What makes it strong? Look at the way she can move:

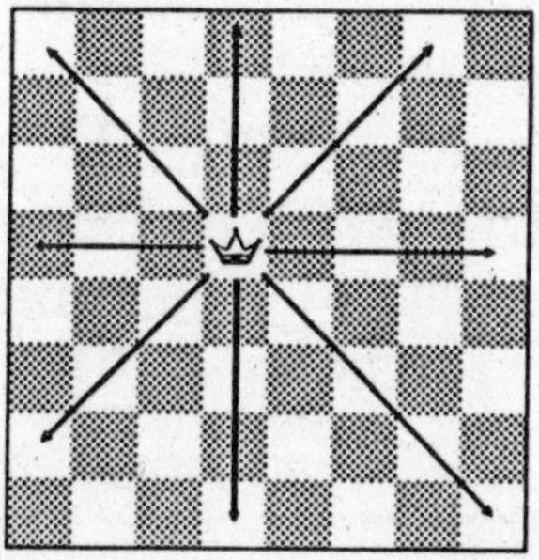

9

She moves along the ranks and files as well as along the diagonals. That is, she has the combined powers of the Rook and the Bishop. Thus she can command 27 squares from her centre position. And any enemy pieces that happen to stumble into her far-sweeping line of fire can be captured. Let us now consider how the Queen captures.

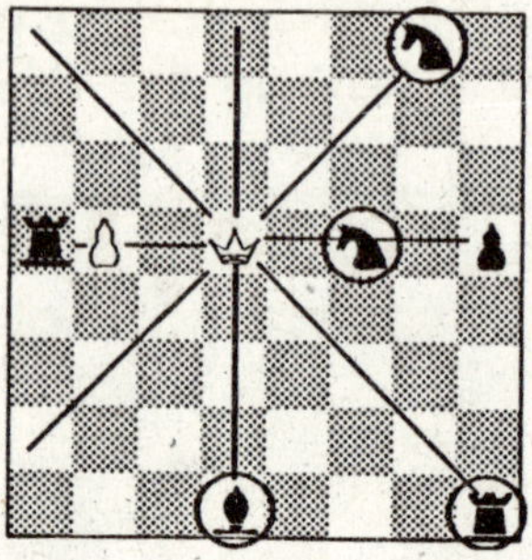

10

In the above shown board, the Queen can capture either of the Black Knights—the one lying at the diagonal and the other on a rank. She can capture the Bishop, which is in her line of fire on a file. And she can also capture one of the Black Rooks along a diagonal. It is due to Queen's this all pervasive power that no player would want to give up his Queen in return for a Bishop or a Rook. So, when the Queen is attacked by a lesser piece which is well protected, you have no go but to make your Queen beat an ignoble retreat.

In the diagram shown below, the Queen can capture any of the five Pawns but not the pieces standing beyond them, as this would involve jumping over the Pawns which no piece except the Knight can do. That will be explained later.

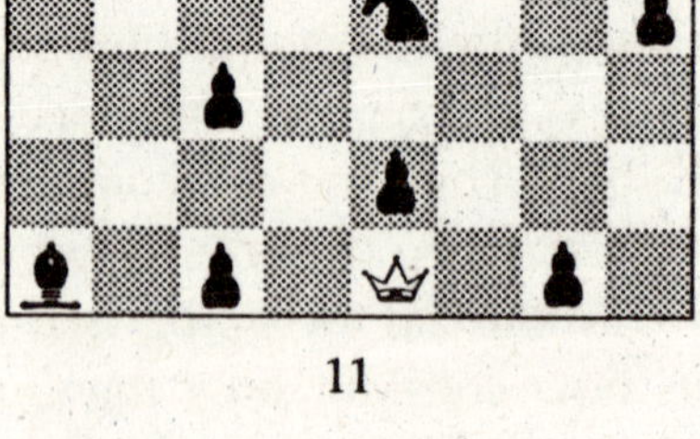

11

(d) **The Knight:** Known in German as the der Springer—the jumper or vaulter, the Knight has the power to jump over his own or enemy pieces. He does not jump in the sense what a checker piece does; that is, he does not capture what he jumps over. He only captures the piece that occupies the square on which he lands. He is a great one for operating in close quarters; he can literally leap into the middle of things, and if the going gets too rough, leap right out again. See the following diagrams to know how a Knight moves.

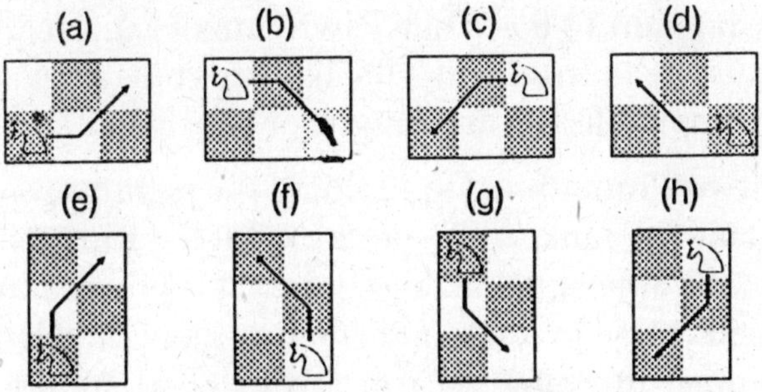

12

Thus the Knight moves one square along a rank or file, then one square along a diagonal. This gives him eight ways to move: right and up (a); right and down (b); left and down (c); left and up (d); up and right (e); up and left (f); down and right (g); and down and left (h).

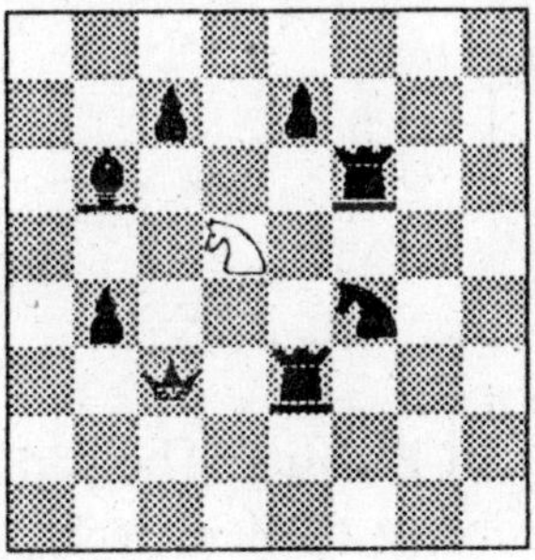

13

Notice that in the preceding diagram the Knight has a choice of eight different captures; corresponding to the eight squares to which he can move. When the Knight captures he, too, replaces the captured piece.

(e) **The Pawn:** We have seen that pieces move in all directions. Pawns move only straight ahead, and one square at a time, except that on its first move each Pawn has the option of moving either one or two squares. Another difference is that the Pawn does not capture with its ordinary move. It captures diagonally forward. Thus in the diagram 14 the White Pawn cannot capture the piece immediately in front of it—the Bishop—but can take either of the other pieces, the Knight or the Black Pawn.

Pawn Promotion: On reaching the eighth row a Pawn must take the rank of any piece except the King. Naturally a Queen is almost invariable choice. This promotion means a huge increase in force, and is much more important than 'Crowning' in draughts. You can make a Pawn a Queen even though your original Queen is on the board. This calls for a cotton reel or an inverted Rook.

Promotion takes effect at once. Thus, in diagram 15 below, White can capture the Knight with his Pawn which at once becomes the Queen to mate Black in just this move.

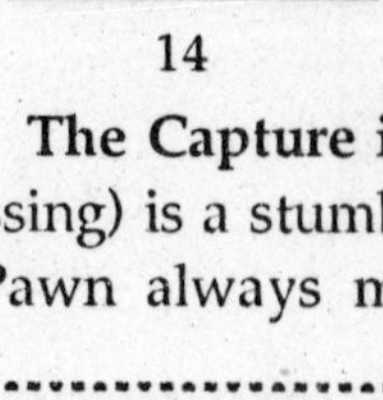

14

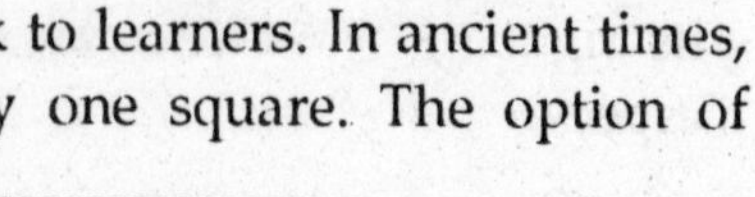

15

The Capture in Passing: The capture 'en passant' (in passing) is a stumbling block to learners. In ancient times, a Pawn always moved only one square. The option of moving it two squares forward on its first move was introduced seven centuries ago to speed up the opening.

Now look at the diagram (i) below. The White Pawn has not yet moved, and therefore has the option of moving either one or two squares. If it moves one square, obviously the Black Pawn can capture it. But the "new" rule (about 1250 AD), allowing it to move two squares, enabled it to evade capture [see the diagram (ii)]. In this way it was found possible for the defending player to block up the board with Pawns, facilitating a draw and making a game tedious.

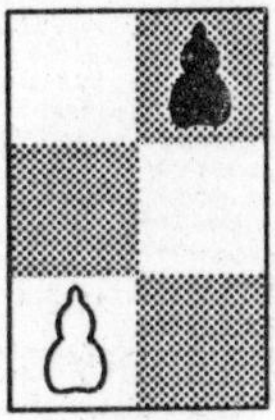

(i)

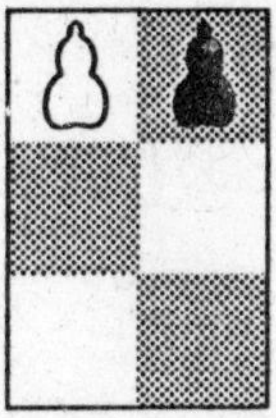

(ii)

(iii)

16

To prevent this, the French chess authorities of the fifteenth century invented a very valuable rule. They permitted the opponent in such a position to capture the White Pawn just as though it had moved only one square. The resulting position has been shown in the diagram (iii) above.

This is called taking "en passant" (in passing). It is not compulsory, but if Black wishes to do it he must do on the reply-move. He cannot make another move and take the Pawn later on. Only a Pawn on the 5th rank if White, 4th rank if Black, can take in passing. According to this rule only a Pawn can be taken, and only when it has used its right to move two squares on its first move i.e. this especial power must be exercised by capturing side on its very next move following the two-squares-forward Pawn move. If the capture is not made then the privilege of capturing that Pawn en passant (abbreviation e.p.) stands forfeited.

(f) **The King:** The King moves in any direction like the Queen, but only one square at a time. Thus the King can move in any direction along a rank, file or diagonal, forward or backward. Only in special circumstances it can move to more squares which shall be discussed under the sub-heading castling. He can capture any piece within this range. But—and this is a big 'hut'—he cannot move into the line of fire of any enemy piece.

In the following diagrams the King can move to any of the squares numbered 1 to 8.

17

If an enemy piece occupied one of those squares the King could capture it and take its place—provided that in doing so he did not move into the range of any enemy piece.

Now consider the following diagram wherein a few pieces of Black have been added to the board.

18

In this, the King cannot move to square 1 because he would be moving into a position where Black Pawn or Black Rook could capture him. That square is controlled by the Rook and Pawn and the King cannot move to a square controlled by the enemy. Square 2 is controlled by the Black Knight. Squares 3, 4, 5 are controlled by the Black Queen. Squares 5, 6, 7, 8 are controlled by the Black Rook. It would, however, not mean that the White King is immobilised. He can capture the Black Rook. In case he does so, the board would look like this:

19

The King has replaced the Rook and he is not in the line of fire of any Black pieces.

(g) The Castling: Once in a game, you have a privilege of moving two pieces in a single move—the King and one Rook. This is called 'castling'. Castling can be done only *when the King and the Rook have as yet made no move in the game, and have nothing between them.* See the three one rank-diagrams below:

(i)

(ii)

(iii)

20

The King moves two squares towards the Rook with which he is to castle, and the Rook then jumps over the King on the square just beyond him. In the second diagram above White has castled with his King's Rook and in the third diagram he has castled with his Queen's Rook.

However, you cannot castle to get out of check; while castling your King must not, of course, move into check; and the King must not even cross a square in range of an enemy piece. But the Rook may cross such a square (this can happen in castling with the Queen's Rook).

A King which has been checked earlier in the game is still free to castle if he has never moved and is not in check when castling is being considered.

The very purpose of castling is to bring the King away from the centre, where the game is usually opened up, and to bring the Rook to a position where it will not be shut out of play by its own King. Note from the above diagrams that castling with the King's Rook brings the King further from the centre and is therefore usually safer.

Castle always early and keep your King sheltered with Pawns. To be prevented from castling is usually a serious handicap because your King is likely to become exposed.

But the handicap may be infinitesimal if the Queens have been exchanged off. It at least one pair of Rooks and at least two pairs of minor Pieces (Bishops, Knights) have also been exchanged, having your King uncastled and therefore near the centre is usually an asset. So if prevented from castling, seek wholesale exchanges especially of the Queens.

Castling early, usually advisable, however, can be a major blunder if your opponent has a great preponderance of pieces on the wing where you think of castling. In such a case, delay castling or consider castling on the other wing.

21

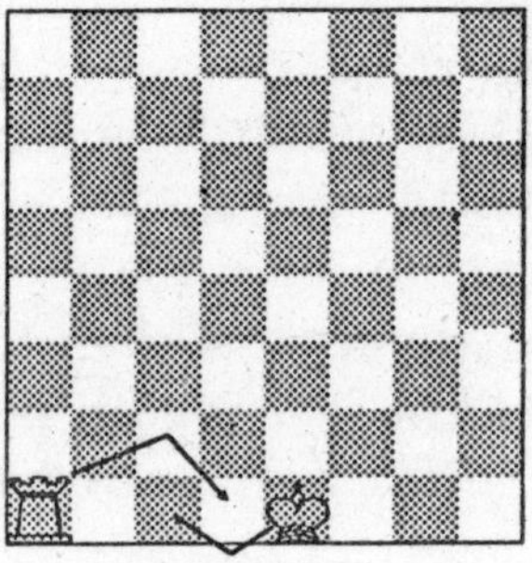

22

Consider the following position on a particular game as shown in the diagram below:

23

In this the White King cannot castle on his Queen's side because the squares between him and the Queen Rook are not clear; the White Knight occupies its home square. He cannot castle King-side either because in doing so he would have to pass through a square which is in the Black Queen's line of fire. Thus the White King, in this position, cannot castle.

The Black King, on the other hand, also cannot castle King-side because his own Bishop is in the way. But there is nothing to stop it from castling on the other side as the rank is clear.

Check and Mate

When a piece moves to a square from which it threatens the enemy King, that piece is said to give check, and the King is "in check". You are not permitted to commit suicide in chess; the King MUST get out of check. It is customary in social chess for the checking player to announce: "Check!". Even if he or she omits to do so, the check remains very much 'on' just the same, and the opponent must get out of it.

There are three possible ways of getting out of check:

(i) Capturing the checking piece;

(ii) Moving the King to a square where it is no longer in check;

(iii) Interposing something between the King and the checking piece. This measure, however, is not effective when the checking piece is the opponent's Knight which has the power to jump over the intervening pieces.

In the first diagram below, Black King is in check and has the choice of all three ways of getting out—one a capture, one (and only one) a King move, and one an interposition. (There is only one King move because others would move the King into check from other units.)

24

If none of these things can be done, it is 'mate', which the player announces (avoiding a triumphant tone obviously)! This brings the game to a close.

Notice in the three diagrams displayed below how Black is mated. Note that in the last diagram below, if the Rook were not protected the King could take it.

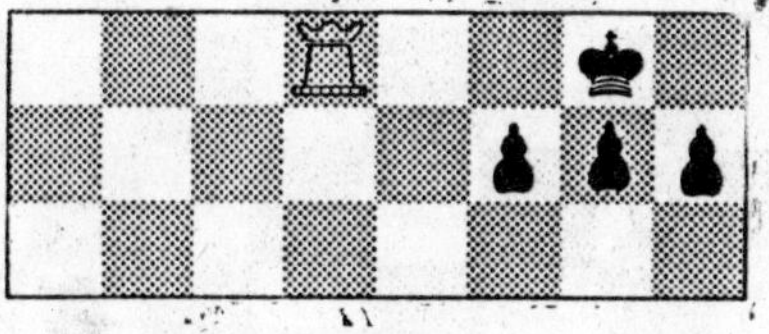

25

26

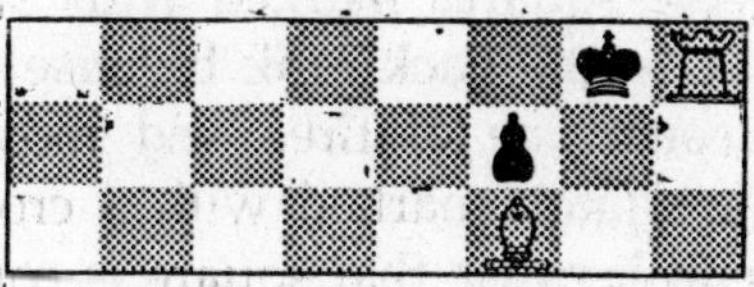

27

If a player makes a move that places his or her King in check the move must be retracted and another made (with the pieces moved if that be legally possible).

As a King can never move into check, it follows that it can never move to a square next to the enemy King. If a King is left in check for even one move, that move and all subsequent moves are void. In case the previous position cannot be replaced, the whole game is replayed.

Let us now consider three examples:

28

In the diagram above the Black King is attacked by the White Bishop. Can he or one of his men capture the Bishop? No. Can a Black piece be moved between the Bishop and the King to shield the King? No. But still, the King is not doomed. He can move to a square that is not under attack—the squares marked with 'X's. He cannot, of course, move to the back rank because that rank is in the White Queen's line of fire. And moving along the diagonal to the square marked with a cross is futile (as well as not legal) because that square is controlled by the attacking White Bishop.

Let us consider another position:

29

The White King is attacked by one of the Black Rooks. The possible escape squares are occupied by the King's own men—he cannot flee to them. The squares marked with X's are controlled by the second Black Rook and there is no White Piece capable of placing itself between the attacking Rook and the King. But White's Bishop can save its King by capturing the attacking Rook.

Consider another example:

30

The King is attacked by the Black Rook. The two escape squares are occupied, one by the White Bishop, one by the White Pawn. There is no way to capture the Rook. But the King can be saved by interposing—i.e. by moving a man between himself and the attacking piece. The Pawn, of course, able to move forward only, is of no use. But the Bishop can be moved to the square marked 'X', shielding the King from the Rook.

When the King is attacked by a Pawn or a Knight there can be no interposing, of course. In the case of such an attack the King can be saved only through the capture of the attacking piece or by moving out of the attacking piece's range.

So, when the King is attacked and it is impossible to get him out of check the game is over. The King has been checkmated and his side lost.

Consider the following position, for example, in which the White King is attacked by the Black Queen. He cannot move to another point on the bottom rank because that entire rank is swept by the Black Queen's line of fire. He cannot flee diagonally to the possible escape squares on

31

the rank above because those squares are occupied by his own Pawns. And he cannot move either to the White square directly above him because he would still be in check—this time by the Black Bishop. There is no way to interpose a White piece between the King and the attacking Queen. And the Queen cannot be captured. Thus the King has no way out of check. He has not been captured—that is, he has not been removed from the board—but he has no way to avoid capture on Black's theoretical next move. The move remains theoretical because the game ends at this point.

III

THE VALUES OF THE PIECES

Although we have already hinted about values each Piece is worth of, now we are giving their comparative details.

Normally over 20 per cent of moves in chess are captures. So, it is vital to have an idea of the average values of the six different units of force.

Each Piece has an average value. For the Queen, Rook and Bishop, it is closely proportionate to the average number of square it controls. An unobstructed Rook always controls 14, but a Bishop's range varies from 13 to 7, and averages just under 9. On that basis a Rook is worth at least 1½ Bishops, and in practice this holds.

Similar calculation would rate a Knight as much weaker than a Bishop, but special factors favour the Knight so much that its true average value approximates to a Bishop's. Factors favouring the Knight are: it cannot be obstructed, and it has access to all 64 squares while a Bishop has only to 32.

In freak positions the average values can be temporarily quite false, but normally they are a good guide. The unit is always taken as an average Pawn, i.e. a Pawn that has no special advantage, like being 'passed' (see ahead) or part of a mating net.

Average values are:

(i) Minor Piece (Bishop or Knight) equals 3 Pawns (3½ in early stages);

(ii) Rook, equals minor Pieces plus 1½ to 2 Pawns;

(iii) Queen equals 2 Rooks or 3 minors; or Rook, minor and 1½ Pawns;

(iv) Summarising it can be said: minor (Knight and Bishop) 3 (3½), Rook 5, Queen 9-10.

In the early stages of the game, the Pawns have various functions. Those in the centre, the most valuable, are used for guarding central squares. Pawns in front of a Castled King are used as a shelter. To wreck the shelter, the enemy often advances Pawns upon yours, to force them to advance or exchange; this operation is called a Pawn-storm. Here the Pawns play the part of tanks rather than infantry.

Pawns sometimes resemble neither tanks nor infantry; their lack of mobility makes them more like natural obstructions (e.g., rivers, hills or marshes) that interfere with mobile warfare. When one of your own Pawns becomes an obstruction to your attack; it often pays to sacrifice it.

A Pawn's value increases as Pieces are exchanged off, for when both armies are so reduced that mate becomes next to impossible, the major objective becomes the 'Queening' of a Pawn. This stage, not reached in all games, is called the end-game; it is for many players the most fascinating part. To be a Pawn ahead with otherwise as good a position as your opponent's, is usually a winning advantage, theoretically.

Passed Pawns: When a Pawn has no enemy Pawn that could hinder it from Queening—that is, no enemy Pawn in front of it on its own file or either of the next-door files—it is called a Passed Pawn. A Passed Pawn in the end-game is a great asset, particularly if well advanced, as the enemy has to use Pieces to stop it Queening, thus reducing their efficiency.

Minor Pieces: Since the Knight can jump over the other pieces, it is good on a crowded board. A Knight 'fork' (called Kainchi in the North Indian colloquial parlance when a Knight gives simultaneous check to the King and threatens the Queen also) is a deadly coup.

A well-posited Knight is as good as well-posited Bishop, but it takes longer for a Knight to get to a good position.

Power of two Bishops: A Bishop is handicapped by being barred from half the squares of the board, since it moves only on squares of one colour. This handicap disappears if its fellow Bishop is still on the board; with open diagonals a team of two Bishops is particularly strong. Because of this, an early èxchange of a Bishop for a Knight is to be avoided unless something is clearly gained.

Value of the Rook: Winning a Rook for a minor piece (a Bishop or a Knight) is called 'winning the exchange'. The exchange is worth, on the average, nearly two Pawns. Two minor pieces equal a Rook and two Pawns for most of the way, but (unless they are two Bishops) only a Rook and one Pawn if the other pieces have been exchanged make the comparative value of Rook increase tremendously. Rooks like the great open spaces and are therefore strongest in the end-game when the board is comparatively clear of the obstructions.

Value of the Queen: Before the end-game, the Queen is worth two Rooks, but in the end-game, the two Rooks are nearly always worth a Pawn more, unless the Rooks' King is exposed to checks.

Another approximate equivalent of a Queen is three minor Pieces e.g. two Knights and a Bishop are almost always at least equal to a Queen, and two Bishops and a Knight are usually superior. Rook plus Bishop (or Knight) plus two Pawns are always almost superior to a Queen. Exception to these valuations occur where the King of the army opposing the Queen is very exposed, so the Queen can recognise many checks, giving itself virtually several successive moves while the opponent is powerless to make useful replies.

About the King: Since the fate of the game hangs on the King, it cannot be given a numerical value. However, when so many pieces have been exchanged that mate is no longer a serious danger, it may and indeed must be used as a fighting piece. As such it rates well below a Rook but above a Bishop or Knight.

When most of the fighting pieces (i.e. pieces other than Pawns) have been exchanged, including the Queens and at least one pair of Rooks, your King ceases to need shelter of Pawns in a corner. Use him as a marauder right in the enemy lines. As mentioned under the sub-heading 'Castling' having your King uncastled and therefore near the centre is usually an asset when the Rooks, Queens and one pair of the minor pieces have been exchanged off.

IV

NOTATIONS TO DEPICT POSITIONS AND MOVES

Chess, being a game of pure intelligence and powerful imagination, has ever remained the beloved of intelligent persons. So they devised a system of enjoying the game even if they are absent. That system is writing notations for the moves. Like music has its notations to make the lovers of music enjoy Beethoven's symphonics even after a century or two, the same way the chess lovers developed the notations for the game to allow the posterity to marvel at the intelligence of the past champions.

Now this system has been perfected so much that you can play the chess or enjoy the game without the chess board being laid before you. For the notations write the moves in your mind. Moreover, you can neither need the rest of this book or make progress at chess, without being able to read chess moves.

There are basically two main systems of notation: the Descriptive and Algebraic. The basic principles of descriptive notations—the system most commonly used, despite its drawbacks—were known and used as far back as the tenth century. It was only in the last hundred years, however, that abbreviations came to be used and standardised.

I. The Descriptive Notation

The moment you set up the board with all the pieces to start the game, you notice that because King faces King and Queen faces Queen, an imaginary line can be drawn down the centre of the board, seperating the King and his pieces from the Queen and her forces. Reading across the bottom rank from the Queen's side to the King's we get the following lineup:

Queen Rook	(abbreviated QR)
Queen Knight	(abbreviated QN)
Queen Bishop	(abbreviated QB)
Queen	(abbreviated Q)
King	(abbreviated K)
King Bishop	(abbreviated KB)
King Knight	(abbreviated KN)
King Rook	(abbreviated KR)

The Pawns are named for the pieces that stand behind them. Thus reading along the second rank, again from the Queen's side to the King's, we have:

Queen Rook Pawn	(QRP)
Queen Knight Pawn	(QNP)
Queen Bishop Pawn	(QBP)
Queen Pawn	(QP)
King Pawn	(KP)
King Bishop Pawn	(KBP)
King Knight Pawn	(KNP)
King Rook Pawn	(KRP)

The files are also named after the pieces that originally occupy their position. So, White's extreme right-hand file, then, is the King Rook (KR) file. This is also Black's KR file, though, it is, of course on Black's extreme left-hand side. White's extreme left-hand file is the QR file; it is also Black's QR file though Black again sees it as his extreme right-hand file.

With the result, the files have the same names from both the Black and White points of view. The ranks, however, do not have because White's first rank is Black's eighth and vice-versa. Suppose you want to describe the following squares:

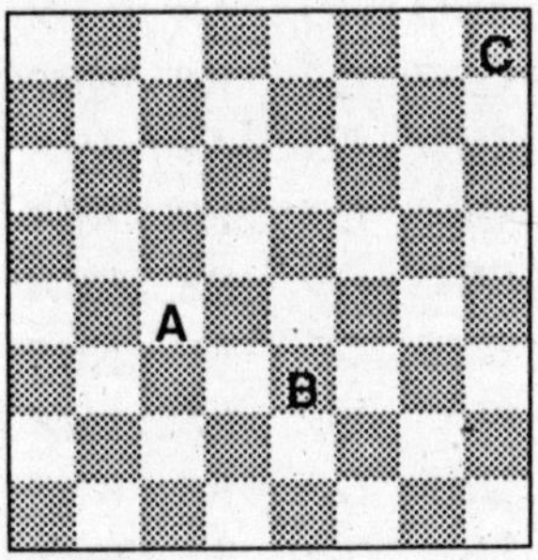

32

We know that square A lies on the Queen Bishop file for both White and Black. From White's point of view—White is always, by custom depicted to be occupying the bottom position at the diagram—the square is four ranks from the bottom. For White, then, square A is Queen Bishop 4 (abbreviated QB4). From Black's point of view, however, it is five ranks from the bottom. Put the diagram upside down to follow this point more clearly. And thus square A is Black's Queen Bishop 5, or QB5.

Square B is on the King file for both White and Black. Looked at from White's side, it is three ranks from the bottom, making is K3. Looked at from Black's side it is six rows up, making it K6.

Square C is on White's last, or eighth, rank and therefore is White's KR8. But it is on Black's first rank, making it Black KR1.

Thus, you find that for every square on the board there are two designations—one from White's side and other from Black's side. The board with these designations depicted from the point of view of White and Black would look like the diagram shown below.

BLACK

QR1 QR8	QN1 QN8	QB1 QB8	Q1 Q8	K1 K8	KB1 KB8	KN1 KN8	KR1 KR8
QR2 QR7	QN2 QN7	QB2 QB7	Q2 Q7	K2 K7	KB2 KB7	KN2 KN7	KR2 KR7
QR3 QR6	QN3 QN6	QB3 QB6	Q3 Q6	K3 K6	KB3 KB6	KN3 KN6	KR3 KR6
QR4 QR5	QN4 QN5	QB4 QB5	Q4 Q5	K4 K5	KB4 KB5	KN4 KN5	KR4 KR5
QR5 QR4	QN5 QN4	QB5 QB4	Q5 Q4	K5 K4	KB5 KB4	KN5 KN4	KR5 KR4
QR6 QR3	QN6 QN3	QB6 QB3	Q6 Q3	K6 K3	KB6 KB3	KN6 KN3	KR6 KR3
QR7 QR2	QN7 QN2	QB7 QB2	Q7 Q2	K7 K2	KB7 KB2	KN7 KN2	KR7 KR2
QR8 QR1	QN8 QN1	QB8 QB1	Q8 Q1	K8 K1	KB8 KB1	KN8 KN1	KR8 KR1

WHITE

In the above diagram the bottom figure in each square is the White Designation; the top figure (to be looked upside down) is the Black's. Since each square needs at least two designations, this becomes the principal drawback of the descriptive notation. The double designation for each square is not the only weakness of the descriptive notation. Since each side has eight Pawns, two Knights, two Bishops and two Rooks, a move, if not notated carefully, can be quite ambiguous or misleading. In the diagram below, for example, the move B-N5 for White can be interpreted two ways: it can mean QB to KN5 or KB to QN5.

34

So, in order to make the move clear, we must specify which Bishop is to be moved. In case we want to move the King Bishop to QN5 we would notate the move as B-QN5 or as KB-N5. It is not necessary to write KB-QN5 because once we specify either the piece or the square to which it should go we have made our move clear. More about this system's drawbacks after we have learnt about the Algebraic notation.

Other Symbols:

—	moves to
×	captures or takes
+	Check (Algebraic notation)
Ch.	Check (Descriptive notation)
++	Checkmate
O-O	Castles (Kingside)
O-O-O	Castles (Queenside)
e.p.	en passant (in passing)
!	best move
!!	beautiful move

?	an error
??	blunder
!?	bold but unsound
- - -	indicates that the following move is made by Black, e.g., 1 . . . e7-e5

II. Algebraic Notation

The diagram below shows how Algebraic notation works. It is now compulsory at all international tournaments and many local chess associations insist on it being adhered to.

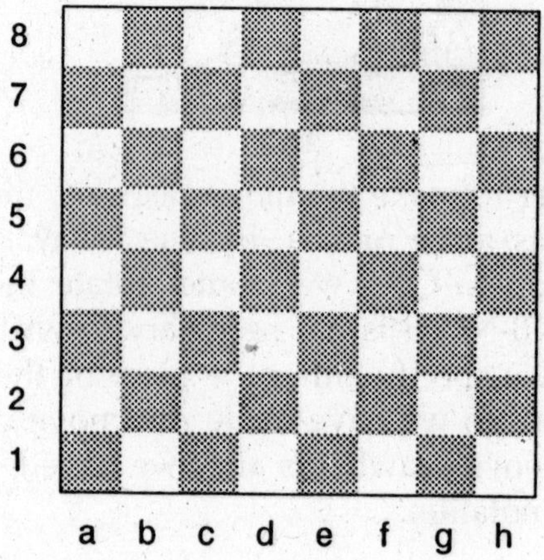

In it the files (vertical lines), from White's left to right, i.e. Black's right to left, are lettered a, b, c, d, e, f, g, h (small letters only are used). Herein the obvious drawback is the similarity of c and e in small print.

The ranks (cross rows) are numbered always from White's side, 1 to 8.

The name of each square is the letter designating the file followed by the number of the rank.

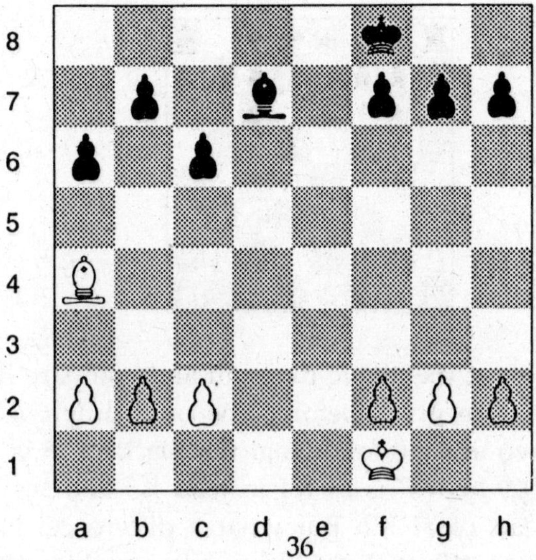

36

The diagram above shows the following position of White pieces: King on f1, Bishop on a4, Pawns (left to right) a2, b2, c2, f2, g2, h2. For Black pieces: King f8, Bishop d7, Pawns a6, b7, c6, f7, g7, h7. Sometimes the Pawn move is also shown by writing e-5 or e-4 which means the Pawn on e file has moved to the fifth square or fourth square from the bottom side (White).

In Algebraic notation the symbol letter of the piece is followed by the square it leaves and the square it moves to. In abbreviated algebraic only the destination square is given, except where there could be ambiguous. For instance, if two Knights could go to g6—one from e5, the other from h4—the move must be written as either Neg6 or Nhg6. If the Knights were on e5 and e7 the move would be written either N5g6 or N7g6. The same rule applies to the moves or Rooks if either Rook could go to the same square.

This clarity of the Algebraic notation makes it more acceptable over the descriptive notation.

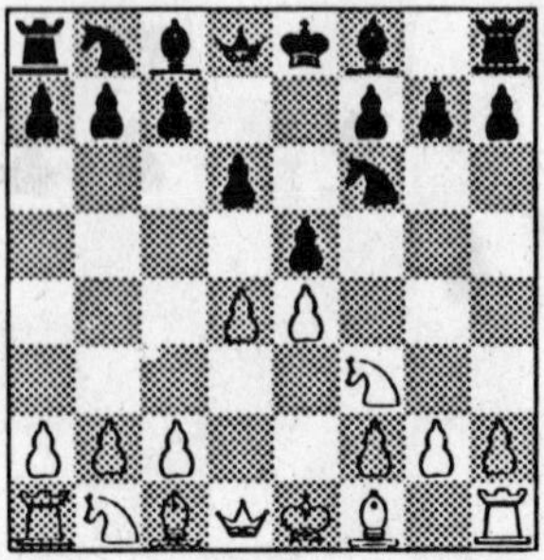

37

Now look at the above diagram and compare it with the 34th diagram given before. The only differences between the two are the following: the Black's QP is at Q3 instead of Q2, his KP is at K4 instead K3 and his KB is at KB1 instead of at K2. But what a difference! Now if we see B-N5 for White it can mean only one thing: Bishop to King Knight 5. Why? Because Bishop to Queen Knight 5 would check the Black King and the move would be B-N5 Ch. The abbreviation Ch- or the lack of it makes the move clear. Only the QB can move to N5 without giving the check.

The real advantage of the Algebraic notation over the descriptive one is the preciseness and clarity. In this any square is designated by the combination of letter-number. White's QN5, for example becomes b5. Black's QN4 is b5

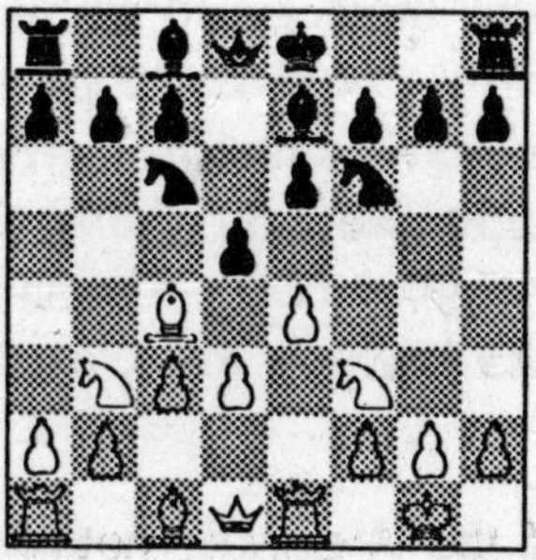

38

too. A move is recorded simply as a starting square and a finishing square—the square from which the piece moves and the square on which it lands. Thus, in the above diagram, the White's move N/QN3-Q4 is written as b-3, d-4. No further clarification is needed. The opening move P-K4 is written simply d4 (no ambiguity here—there is only one piece on the board that can move to K4 at the start of a game).

It is chiefly owing to its less complexity and more clarity that this notation is preferred everywhere. Our advice to the young learners is to learn both the notations. If you leave the descriptive one you shall be depriving yourself of the gems of the chess moves written in descriptive notation by the wizards of chess in earlier period when the Algebraic system was non-existent.

In both notations captures are indicated by 'X' but many continental players use a colon, e.g. g5 : f6 or f6: (in abbreviated form). In either case the captured piece is not mentioned. Sometimes in abbreviated Algebraic the 'X' is omitted, especially when a Pawn captures, e.g. dXe4 is written de4.

Algebraic notation is now used by all nations, which use their own symbols for the pieces. The nearest thing to an international language in chess is German. The German symbols for pieces are K (for Koenig or King), D (Dame, or Queen) etc. See the details about the various symbols used in chess notations by various countries, although most of them adhere to the German symbols.

In books and magazines which cater for readers from different nations, pictorial symbols (given in the IInd Chapter) instead of letters are used. (See the chart ahead)

ENGLISH	King K	Queen Q	Rook R	Bishop B	Knight N or Kt	Pawn P
HINDI	Badshah बा	Vazir व	Haathi ह	Oont ऊँ	Ghorah घ	Paidal प
GERMAN	Koenig K	Dame D	Turm T	Laufer L	Springer S	Bauer B
FRENCH	Roi KR	Dame D	Tour T	Fou F	Cavalier C	Pion P
RUSSIAN	Korolj KP	Ferz ф	Ladia Λ	Slon C	Konj K	Pechka П
SPANISH	Rey R	Dama D	Torre T	Alfil A	Caballo C	Peon P
ITALIAN	Re R	Donna D	Torre T	Alfiere A	Cavalo C	Pedone P

V

MOBILITY: COMBINATIONS

A Paradox: A Queen is about nine times as valuable as a Pawn, yet an attack by a Pawn is, in general, more dangerous than an attack by a Queen!

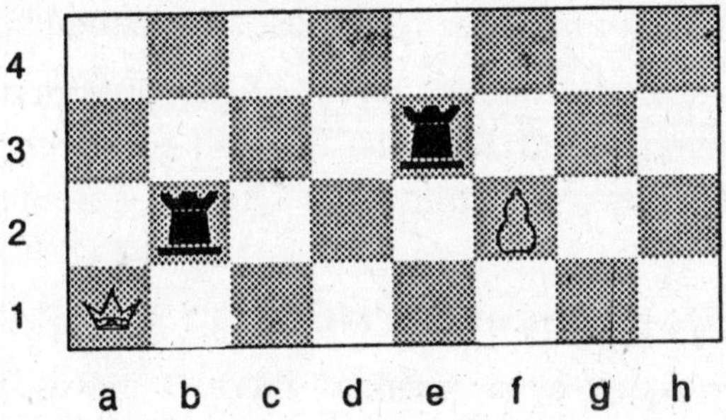

39

In the above diagram, one Rook is being attacked by a Pawn, the other by a Queen. The first Rook must move to avoid to capture, but the second Rook has the choice either moving away or enlisting the other Rook's support, by Re3-e2. If both Rooks were attacked by Pawns, one would fall.

In the diagram below, both Rooks are 'protected', but to the Pawn this means nothing, its attack is just as effective as before. The Queen's 'attack', on the contrary, is now quite illusory for if she captured the Rook, she herself would be taken on the next move.

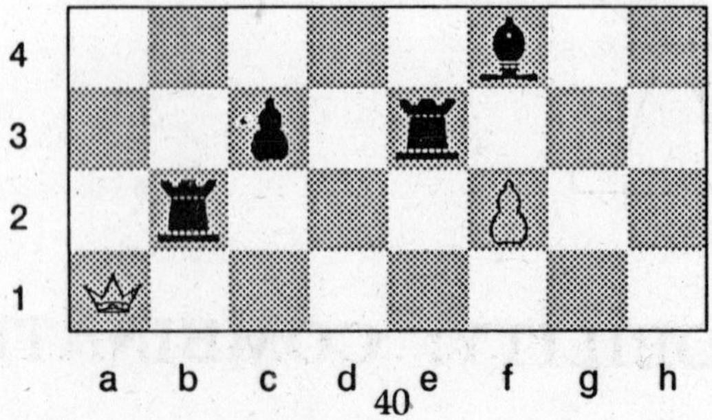

40

This is a very vital element in chess strategy. It means that a larger unit, attacked by a protected smaller unit, must move away if it wishes to save itself. The more warier a piece the warier you must be of exposing it to attack. Your forces are like a fleet; battleships and heavy cruiser must not by unnecessarily exposed to danger.

For example, while several of the opponent's minor pieces (Bishops and Knights) are still on the board, it is usually a mistake to bring your Queen or Rooks into the open.

Always remember that MOBILITY IS PARAMOUNT.

If an attack by a 'weaker' Piece is more dangerous, where lies the value of the 'stronger' Piece? The answer is simply: MOBILITY—that is, freedom of movement.

The vast importance of mobility is most clearly seen when a Piece is, for any reason, deprived of mobility, that is, confined to a very few squares, or still worse, unable to move at all. Such a Piece is a target for attack, and is often doomed to destruction.

Various ways in which individual units may be destroyed through lack of mobility are now shown. To be able to see such possibilities, for and against actual play, is the most essential element in chess skill. Coups of these kinds are called combinations. A sound combination forces an advantage against any defence; it is not a mere trap.

The Net

The simplest case is that of a Piece whose lines of retreat are cut off. This Piece may be said to be in a 'net'.

41

In the above diagram we have the common case of a Knight which has captured a Rook in the enemy's corner. Both the squares commanded by the Knight, viz. f7 and g6, are guarded by the enemy, who has only to bring his remaining Rook to bear on the Knight e.g. by Ke8-e7 to capture it.

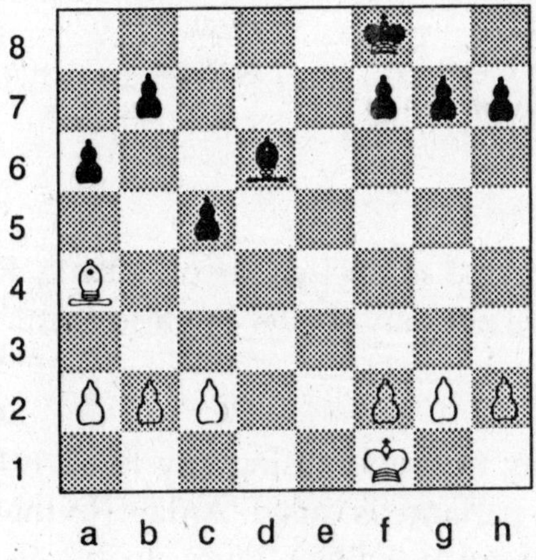

42

The diagram above shows a doomed Bishop. This Piece has its retreat cut off not by enemy units but its own Pawns. Thus:

White	*Black*
1. ...	b7-b5
2. Ba4-b3	c5-c4

and the Bishop falls. Had White foreseen this in time, the line of retreat could have been opened by playing c2-c3.

In fact Mate is a 'net' with the King as victim. In this case the 'net' may be tightened by a sacrifice, often the Queen. Thus, in the diagram below, White finishes very prettily.

White	*Black*
1 Qe6 – g8 + !!	**Rd8xg8**
2 Nh6–f7 + + !	

Black was forced to encircle its own King. Remember that a King needs not only shelter but also a little freedom.

The Pin

Another way of immobilising any Piece is by a 'Pin' which in Indian parlance is called 'Ardab'. In the following two diagrams there is a Black Piece unable to move off the threatened line because to do so would put its King in check.

In the first diagram the pinning Piece itself will give the death-blow; in the second one White will play d4-d5 and the executioner will be a Pawn. The Knight is 'protected' by a Pawn, but this does not help as we will explain later.

44

45

Note that in first diagram White could take the Rook at once and win 'the Exchange' (Rook for minor Piece). But much better is Ke5-e6!, first winning a whole Rook next move.

In the first diagram above some beginners think that White might equally play Ke5-f6. This is illogical. A unit (here the Rook) retains its checking power even though completely pinned. Careful thought will show this to be quite logical.

The Fork

Yet another way a Piece may fatally lose its mobility is through a 'fork', a simultaneously attack on two Pieces.

46

In the diagram above the Knight has simultaneously checked the Black King and threatened the Queen; the Queen is deprived of mobility for one move and is lost. Failure to force this possibility in actual play will spell disaster.

The Skewer

Another type of combination sometimes called a 'skewer' is shown in diagram below:

47

Here White wins Queen for Rook by checking with the Rook.

Tied Piece

A piece may also be deprived of its mobility by being tied to some defensive task. In the diagram 48, a Knight is shown tied to the defence of a Rook. White simply attacks the Knight with a Pawn, and either the Knight or the Rook must fall.

48

Note that a Knight is the worst piece for defence, as it cannot move away and still maintain the defence. If a Bishop were defending the Rook in the above diagram, and a Pawn attacked the Bishop, the Bishop might be able to move another square on the same diagonal where it could still defend the Rook.

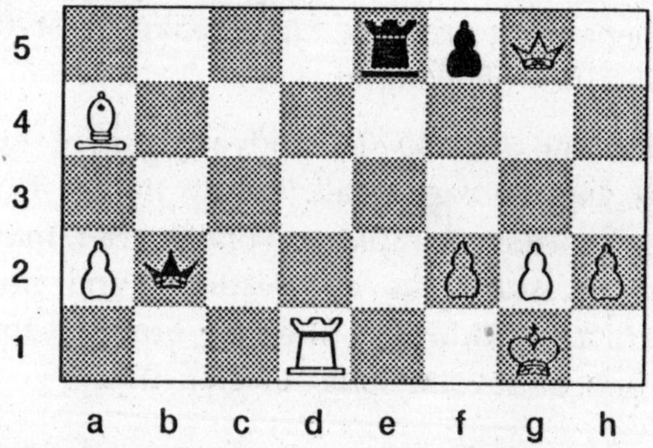

The diagram above shows a subtler example. Here the White Rook is tied to the back rank because if it went away the Black Rook would mate. This gives Black the opportunity for a pretty coup: Qb2-d4. The Rook cannot take the Queen, so the Queen is in effect forking the White Rook and Bishop. Black after....Qb2-d4 is threatening, then ...Qd4×dl; Ba4×dl, Re5-el mate!

Such positions should be avoided by moving a Pawn one square to make an escape for the King, for example by h2-h3.

FROM THESE EXAMPLES—REMEMBER—THAT USING A PIECE FOR DEFENCE IS ITSELF A DISADVANTAGE.

A Cramped Game

Lack of mobility does not always lead to rapid disaster, as the enemy may not have the means of reaping a quick advantage. But it is always disadvantageous as it limits one's possibilities both of a attack and defence.

Always remember that you should never attempt to take advantage of an opponent's cramped position by attacking it. For the attack may free the enemy. Rather concentrate on preserving and increasing the cramp prevent freeing moves. The cramp should grow to a point where your opponent must create a fatal weakness or make a desperate sacrifice of material.

Mobility for Attack: The advantages of superior mobility are limitless. A small, highly mobile force, by being able to concentrate rapidly in one quarter, may effect mate against a numerous but scattered and immobile enemy. Such a position can often be brought about by sacrificing one or several units to gain time.

Mobility and the Centre

As a general rule, whoever controls the greater share of the centre has the greater mobility. The centre may be said to consist of the 16 most central squares of the board, and especially the four square in the very centre, viz. e4, d4, e5, and d5.

In the centre, Queens, Bishops and Knights have greater mobility than elsewhere and can move rapidly to either wing as occasion demands.

VI

LAWS OF CHESS

PART I

GENERAL LAWS

Introduction

The game of chess is played by two opposing players by moving pieces on a square board called a 'chessboard'.

ARTICLE 2

The Chessboard and its Arrangement

1. The chessboard is made up of 64 equal squares in colour alternatively light and dark. ("white". and "black" squares respectively).

2. The chessboard is placed between the players in such a way that the square in the corner to the right of each player is white.

3. The eight rows of squares running from one player to the other are called "files".

4. The eight rows of squares running at right angles to the files are called "ranks".

5. The rows of squares of the same colour touching at comers are called "diagonals".

The initial position of the pieces on the chessboard is as follows:

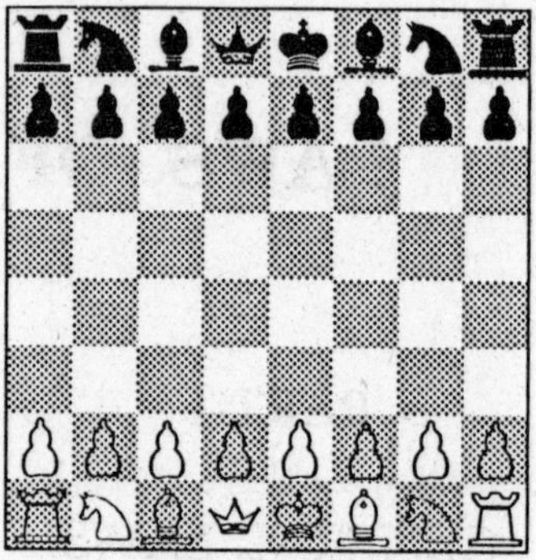

49

ARTICLE 3

The Pieces and their Positions

At the beginning of the game one player has 16 light coloured pieces (the "White" pieces), the other has 16 dark coloured pieces (the "Black" pieces).

These pieces on each side are as follows: a King, a Queen, two Rooks, two Bishops, two Knights and eight Pawns.

ARTICLE 4

The Method of Play

1. The two players shall play alternatively and make one move at a time. The player with the White pieces commences the game.
2. A player whose turn it is to play is said "to have the move".

ARTICLE 5

The Move in General

1. With the exception of a castling (Article 6) a move is the transfer of a piece from one square to another which is either unoccupied or occupied by an opponent's piece.

2. No piece, except the Rook when castling or the Knight (Article 6), can cross a square occupied by another piece.

3. When a piece is played to a square occupied by an opponent's piece, the opponent's piece is said to have been "captured" and it is immediately removed from the chessboard by the player who has made the capture. See Article 6(b) for taking **"en passant"**.

ARTICLE 6

These Pieces are as follows: (for White Player)

♔	A King	♕	A Queen
♖	Two Rooks	♗	Two Bishops
♘	Two Knights	♙	Eight Pawns

The Moves of the Individual Pieces

The King: Except when castling, the King moves to an adjacent square that is not attacked by an opponent's piece. Castling is a move of the King and a Rook, counting as a single move (of the King) carried out in the following manner. The King is transferred from its original square to either of the two squares of the same colour nearest in the same rank, then the Rook towards which the King has been moved is transferred over the King to the square which the King has just crossed.

Castling is permanently impossible: (a) if the King has already been moved, or (b) with a Rook that has already been moved.

Castling is prevented for the time being: (a) if the original square of the King or the squares which the King must cross or that which it is to occupy is attacked by an opponent's piece, or (b) if there is any piece between the Rook involved in the move and the King.

The Queen: The Queen moves to any square on the rank, file, or either of the diagonals on which it stands.

The Rook: The Rook moves to any square on the rank or file on which it stands.

The Bishop: The Bishop moves to any square on either of the diagonals on which it stands.

The Knight: The Knight's move is made up of two different steps. It takes one step of single square along the file or rank, and then, still moving away from the square it left, takes one step along a diagonal. (Note: Another simple way of remembering the Knight's move is to consider it as moving the diagonal of a rectangle of 3 × 2 squares).

The Pawn: The pawn can only move forward.

(a) Except when making a capture, it advances from its original square either one or two vacant squares along the file on which it stands, and on subsequent moves it advances one vacant square along the file. When making a capture it advances one square along either of the diagonals on which it stands.

(b) A Pawn attacking a square crossed by an opponent's Pawn which has been advanced two squares on the previous move can capture the opponent's Pawn as though the latter had only been moved one Square. This can only be made on the move immediately following such advance and is known as taking **"en passant"**.

(c) On reaching the eighth rank the Pawn must immediately as part of the same move be exchanged for a Queen, a Rook. A Bishop or a Knight at the player's choice without taking into account the other pieces still remaining on the chessboard. This exchanging of a Pawn is called "promotion". The promoted piece must be of the same colour as the Pawn and its action is immediate.

ARTICLE 7

The Completion of a Move

A move is completed:

(a) In the case of the transfer of a piece to a vacant square, when the player's hand has quitted the piece; or

(b) In the case of a capture, when the captured piece has been removed from the chessboard and when the player, having placed the piece on its new square, has quitted the piece with his hand; or

(c) In the case of a castling, when the player's hand has quitted the Rook on the square crossed by the King; when the player's hand has quitted the King the move is still incomplete but the player has no longer the right to make any other move except castling; or

(d) In the case of promotion of a Pawn, when the Pawn has been removed from the chessboard and the player's hand has quitted the new piece after placing it on the promotion square; if the player's hand has quitted the Pawn that has reached the promotion square the move is still incomplete but the player no longer has the right to move the Pawn to another square.

ARTICLE 8

Touched Piece

Provided that he first warns his opponent the player whose turn it is to move may adjust one or more pieces on their squares.

Apart from the above case, if the player whose turn it is to move touches one or more pieces he must make his move by moving or taking the piece first touched which can be moved or taken.

The touching of a piece or pieces entails no obligation if a breach of this rule is not pointed out by the opponent before he touches a piece, or if none of the moves indicated above can be carried out in accordance with the rules.

ARTICLE 9

Illegal Positions

1. If, during the game, it is found out that an illegal move has been made, then the position shall be reconstructed as it was immediately before the illegal move was played. The game shall then continue in accordance with the rules given in Article 8 as regards the move replacing the illegal move.

If it proves impossible to reconstruct the position, then the game shall be annulled and a fresh game played.

2. If during a game, one or more pieces have been accidentally displaced and are not correctly replaced, the position shall be set up as it was immediately before the mistake and the game continued.

   If it proves impossible to set up the position again, the game shall be annulled and a fresh game started.

3. If, after on adjournment, the position is incorrectly put up, then the position as it was on adjournment shall be set up again and the game continued.

4. If, during a game, it is found that the initial position of the pieces was incorrect, then the game shall be annulled and a fresh game played.

   (F.I.D.E. Interpretation—This has been extended to apply to the case where the players have started with the wrong colours).

5. If, during a game it is found that the position of the chessboard is incorrect, then the position reached shall be transferred to a chessboard correctly placed and the game continued.

   (F.I.D.E. Interpretations—All irregularities cited in Article 9 are ignored if discovered after a game has in fact ended. But, within a reasonable time after the agreed "end" of the game, it may be proved that it had in fact ended earlier, e.g., by an unnoticed mate or stalemate or by a valid but incorrectly disallowed claim of a draw or an exceeding of the time limit. (Article 17). Any moves or agreements that occurred after the game did in fact end, are null and void. The F.I.D.E. has also ruled that an unfinished game subject to adjudication is not finished until adjudicated).

ARTICLE 10

Check

1. The King is in check when the square it occupies is attacked by an opponent's piece; the latter is said to be "checking the King".

2. The check must be warded off on the move immediately following. If the check cannot be avoided then it is "mate" (see Article 11-1).

3. A piece that intercepts a check to its King can itself give check to the opponent's King.

ARTICLE 11

Won Game

1. The game is won for the player who has mated the opponent's King.

2. The game is considered won for the player whose opponent declares he resigns.

ARTICLE 12

Drawn Game

1. When the King of the player whose turn it is to move is not in check, and the player cannot make a legal move, situation is called "stalemate".

2. By agreement between the two players (see Article 17A).

3. On demand by one of the players when the same position appears three times, the same player having the move each time. The position is considered the same if pieces of the same kind and colour occupy the same squares, and the possible moves of all pieces are unchanged.

   This right of claiming the draw belongs only to the player:

   (a) who is in a position to play a move leading to such repetition of the position, if he indicates this move and claims the draw before making it; or

   (b) who is due to reply to a move by which such repeated position has been produced, provided he does not move before claiming.

   If a player's claim of a draw under clause (a) proves incorrect (Article 17A) and the game continues, that player is still bound to play the move he indicated.

   If a player makes a move without having claimed a draw in the manner prescribed in (a) or (b) he then loses his right to claim a draw; this right is, however, restored to him if the same position appears again with the same player having the move, and with the possible moves of all pieces unchanged.

4. When the player whose turn it is to move proves that at least fifty moves have been played by each side without a capture of a piece and without a Pawn-move having been made.

This number of fifty moves can be increased for certain positions provided the number is clearly laid down before the start of the game.

Addenda—Article 8

Supplementary to Paragraph 1—Should the opponent be absent, a player who wishes to adjust one or more pieces may do so after giving notice to the umpire.

ARTICLE 12

F.I.D.E. Interpretations—A player is not entitled to claim a draw "by perpetual check" until he can do so under Section 3. A player is not entitled to claim a draw because it is impossible for his opponent to mate; he must continue to play if none of Sections 1 to 4 apply, and he could lose under Article 17 (see Part II).

PART II

ADDITIONAL RULES FOR COMPETITIONS

ARTICLE 13

Recording of Games

1. During the play, each player is required to record the game (moves of his own and his opponent's), move by move, as clearly and legibly as possible on the score-sheet provided for the contest.

2. If, acutely pressed for time, a player is clearly unable to comply with the Section 1 above, he shall nevertheless do his best to indicate on his score-sheet the number of moves made. As soon as his

time trouble is over he shall immediately complete his record of the game by writing down the omitted moves. But he shall not have the right to claim a draw under Article 12, Section 3 if the moves in question were not recorded in conformity with Section 1 above.

F.I.D.E. Interpretation—

(a) The word "acutely pressed for time" is open for the referee's decision at the spot taking into account the time on the clock, number of moves to be made and the nature of the position at the moment. The referee may decide that a player is not "acutely pressed for time" and require the player to record the moves in conformity with Section 1. If the player refuses, the referee may rule that the player loses the game under Article 17, Section 4.

(b) If, on the referee's instruction to write down the moves, a player declares that he cannot fill the missing moves without consulting his opponent's score-sheet, the request for the sheet shall be made to the referee, who will judge whether the player's form can be completed before the time control without embarrassing the opponent. The latter shall not refuse his score-sheet, for two reasons: The record belongs to the organisers of the contest, and the player who is to complete his record shall do so in his own time.

(c) In all other cases, the score-sheets can be completed only after the time control. There are then two possibilities: One player alone has not completed his record, in which case he shall do so in his own playing time; both players have not completed records, in which case both clocks shall be stopped until the two records are completed, if necessary with the help of a chessboard under the control of the referee, who shall, beforehand, have recorded the position existing at the moment of the interruption. If in the first possibility the referee sees that the player's score-sheet, although filled in, will not help in reconstituting the game, he shall act as in the second possibility.

ARTICLE 14

Use of the Chess Clock

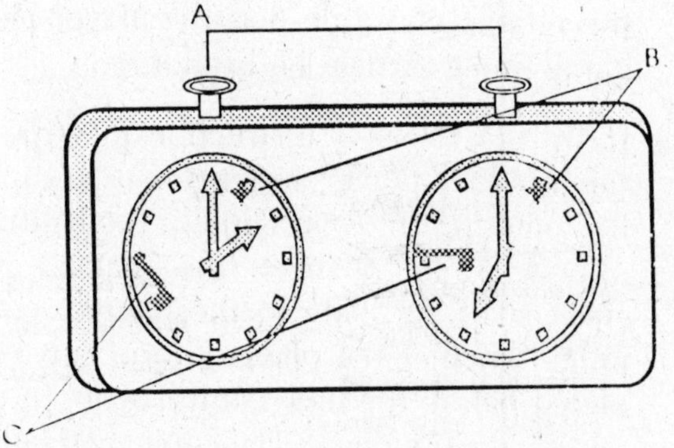

Chess Clock: A player punches one of the two knobs (A) as he finishes making his move. This stops his own clock and starts his opponent's. The "tickers"; (B) show which of the two clocks is running. When a player has used up an hour, the flag (C) drops.

1. Each player has to complete a certain number of moves within a certain time, these two factors having been laid down in advance.**

2. The time control for each player is effected by means of a clock provided with a special apparatus usually a "flag".

3. The clock of the player who has White is set in motion at the time fixed for the commencement of the game. After that, each player, having made his move, stops his clock and starts that of his opponent.

   (F.I.D.E. Interpretation—The first sentence of Section 3 applies even if both players are late).

4. When considering whether the prescribed number of moves has been made in the given time the last move is not considered as made until after the player has stopped his clock.

   [F.I.D.E. Interpretation—Section 4 of Article 14 does not apply if the last move ends the game, e.g. by mate, stalemate, or draw under Article 12; Section 3, clause (a). This is consistent with F.I.D.E. interpretation of Article 9].

5. All indications given by a clock or its apparatus are considered as conclusive in the absence of evident defects. The player who claims that there is such a defect is bound to do so as soon as he becomes aware of it.

   F.I.D.E. Interpretation—The second sentence of Section 5 does not imply that the harm suffered by a player through an evident defect must be rectified retrospectively. For example, if a player shows that his opponent's clock has ceased to function, he is entitled to be provided with a sound clock but not to have the clock times changed.

** Note: Generally the following time limits are observed:

(a) for a five hour session—each player to complete 40 moves in the first 2-1/2 hours (on his clock) and 16 moves per hour thereafter.

(b) for a four hour session—36 moves in the first two hours and 18 moves an hour thereafter.

(c) for a three hour session—32 moves in the first one and a half hour and 20 moves an hour thereafter.

6. If the game has to be interrupted for some reason for which neither player is responsible the clock shall be stopped until the point concerned has been dealt with. This shall be done, for example, in the case of an illegal position necessitating correction, or in that of a defective clock that must be changed, or if a piece for Pawn promotion is not immediately at hand.

7. In cases arising out of Article 9, clauses 1 and 2, when it proves impossible to determine the time taken by each player upto the moment when the illegality occurred, each player shall be allotted up to this moment a time proportional to that indicated on the clock at the moment when the illegality was found out.

ARTICLE 15

Adjournment of the Game

1. If, after the lapse of the time laid down for play, the game is not finished, the player whose turn it is move shall write down his move in unambiguous

notation on his score-sheet, put this score-sheet as well as of his opponent in an envelope, close the envelope and them stop his clock. This move is called the "sealed move". Should the player make his move on the chessboard he shall seal the same move on his score-sheet.

2. On the envelope shall be stated:

   (a) The name of the players.

   (b) The position immediately before the sealed move.

   (c) The time taken by each player.

   (d) The name of the player who has sealed his move and the number of this move.

3. The envelope shall be put in safe custody.

ARTICLE 16

Resumption of the Game

1. When the game is to be resumed position immediately before the sealed move shall be set up and the time taken by each of the players when the game was adjourned shall be indicated on the clocks.

2. The envelops shall not be opened until the player whose turn it is move (i.e. the one who is to reply to the sealed move) is present. The clock of this player shall be started when the sealed move has been made on the chessboard.

3. If the player whose turn it is to move is absent, then his clock shall be started, but the envelope shall be opened only when he arrives.

4. When the player who has sealed the move is absent, then the player whose turn it is to move need not make his reply to the sealed moved on the chessboard. He has the right to write down his move in reply on his score-sheet, put this move in an envelope, stop his clock and start his opponent's clock. The envelope shall then be put into safe custody and opened on the opponent's arrival.

5. If the envelope containing the sealed, move has disappeared without it being possible to re-establish, with the agreement of the two players, the position and the times used for the adjourned game, or if for any other reason the said position and the said times cannot be re-established, the game is annulled and a fresh game shall be played instead of the adjourned game.

   If the envelope enclosing the move sealed according to Sub-Article 4 has disappeared then the game shall be resumed as from the position at the time of the adjournment and with the clock time used at the same time.

6. If, at a resumption of play, either clock has been incorrectly set, and if either player points this out before making his first move, then the error shall be corrected. If the error is not so pointed out the game continues without correction.

ARTICLE 17

Loss of the Game

A game is lost by a player:

1. Who has not played the prescribed number moves in the given time;

2. who arrives at the chessboard more than one hour late, either at the commencement or the resumption;

3. who has sealed a move the real significant of which is impossible to establish;

   (F.I.D.E. Interpretation—If the game has already been ended by agreement or otherwise before the sealed move is opened, the sealed move is null and void).

4. who during the game refuses to comply with the Laws of Chess.

   If both players arrive at the chessboard more than one hour late, or if both refuse to comply with the Laws of Chess, the game shall be declared lost of both.

ARTICLE 17 (DRAWN GAME)

1. A proposal of a draw may be made by a player only at the moment when he has made a move. On proposing a draw he starts his opponent's clock. The opponent may accept or, either orally or by making a move, reject the proposal. In the interval, the player who has made the proposal cannot withdraw it.

ARTICLE 17A, No. 2

2. If a player claims a draw in accordance with Article 12(3) his clock shall run until the Competition Director has investigated the correctness of his claim. If the claim is proved correct, the game shall be declared a draw, even if the claimant has exceeded the time limit in the meantime. If the claim is proved to be incorrect, the game shall be continued, unless the claimant has exceeded the

time limit, in which case the game shall be declared lost for the claimant.

(*Note*: National Federations have the right to forbid, in events of their own, an agreement to a draw before each player had made 30 moves. But this does not apply to F.I.D.E. events. However, referees at all events are expected to impose penalties on players who are guilty of clear violations of the moral principles of chess. In extreme cases the penalty may be loss of the game. A premature agreement to a draw could under certain circumstances come into this category of behaviour).

ARTICLE 18

Players' Behaviour

1. (a) While play is in progress players are forbidden to use written or printed notes or to analyse the game on another chessboard, and are also forbidden to have recourse to the counsel or advice of a third party, whether asked for or not.

   (b) No analysis is allowed in the rooms of play either while play is in progress or during the adjournment.

   (c) It is forbidden to distract or worry the opponent in any way whatsoever.

2. Infringements of the law in Sub-Article 1 may incur penalties extending even to forfeiture of the game.

ARTICLE 19

The Competition Director

A person shall be designated to direct a competition. The ties of this Director are:

(a) to see that the rules of play are strictly observed;

(b) to supervise the competition, to enforce the time control, to fix the order of resumption of adjourned games, to see that arrangements contained, in Article 15 are observed, above all to see that the particulars put down on the envelope at the adjournment are correct, to be custodian of the sealed envelopes until the time when the game is resumed; etc.

(c) to put into force decisions which may be taken by him on disputes that have arisen in the course of the competition;

(d) to impose penalties on the players for any fault or infringement of the rules.

ARTICLE 20

The Interpretation of the Laws of the Game

In case of doubt as to be application or interpretation of these laws the F.I.D.E., will examine the evidence and make an official decision.

CONCLUDING NOTE

The Laws of Chess cannot, should not, cover every possible situation that might occur during play; nor do they cover every question of organisation. In most such cases a correct decision can normally be found by applying, by analogy, the provisions for cases of a similar type. As for the Director's duties, it can only be assumed that in most cases he has the necessary competence, sound judgment and complete objectivity.

In the following cases the decision is left to the Competition Director:

(i) Where a player offers a draw too frequently. (Article 18c may be applied).

(ii) In defining what constitutes evident defects of a clock.

(iii) The procedure where a player or team arrives late for the start of a competition. If the delay is due to a cause for which a player or team is not responsible, it must follow from the principles of chess collaboration at least in international tournaments that concessions should be granted as far as is possible without creating eventual difficulties to other players the organisation.

APPENDIX

CHESS NOTATION

For recording the games the F.I.D.E. rules recognise two systems of notation, namely, the Algebraic notation and the Descriptive notation.

The Algebraic Notation

Here, the pieces, with the exception of the Pawns are represented by their initial letters (the Knight generally by 'N'). The Pawns are not mentioned.

The eight files from the left to right of White are represented by the letters a, b, c, d, e, f, g, h. The eight ranks form White side of the board are numbered 1, 2, 3, 4, 5, 6, 7, 8.

The combination of letters and figures can now designate every square on the board. For example, White's Queen Rook's square will be "a1" and Black's King Rook's square "h8".

While writing the move, the initial letter of the piece (except the Pawn) with the square of departure and arrival will form the unit of the notation. For example, e2-e4 will indicate that the Pawn on e2 has moved to the square e4. Similarly, the notation Nb8-c6 will mean that the Knight from b8 has moved to c6. The **en passant** capture is indicated on the square of capture; thus if White plays his Pawn from h2 to h4 and Black captures **en passant** by his Pawn on h4, then the notations will read: h2-h4, g4xh3. In the shortened form of notation the square of departure is omitted.

When two similar pieces can go to the same square, the shortened notation is completed in the following way: if for example, two Knights are on g1 and d2, the move Ng1-f3 will be written in the shortened form Ng-f3. If the Knights are on g1 and g5, the move Ng1-f3 will be shortened as N1-f3.

The Descriptive Notation

In this, the pieces are represented by their initial letters, including the Pawn which is indicated by the letter P. Here "N" is generally preferred for Knight. Distinction between the King side pieces and the Queen side pieces is made, where necessary, by adding the letters K or Q before the piece mentioned.

The eight files are given the names of the pieces which originally stand on them. That is, reading from left to right the files are (from the White's side) QR, QN, QB, Q, K, KB, KN, KR. For Black the same will be from right to left.

The eight ranks are numbered from 1 to 8 from White's side on the board for White and from Black's side of the board for Black. (Note that there is no such distinction in the Algebraic notation).

The initial letter of the piece moved and the square to which it is moved are indicated. Thus: B-QB4 means the Bishop is played the the Queen Bishop's file on the fourth square. Where two similar pieces can move to the same square, then the square of departure is also mentioned, usually within brackets: the, R(Q2)-K2 means that the Rook on Q2 moves to K2. Or if any piece can move to similar files on either side of the board, distinction is made in the square of arrival by adding the appropriate letter, thus: R-QB2 means that the Rook, which could have moved to either KB2 or QB2 did so to the latter. In other cases simple QB2 might suffice. Similarly if two pieces from different squares can move to the same square, then the square of origin of the piece moved must be indicated as also the square of arrival. For example, the Rooks are on KR2 and QR2 and it is desired to show that the Rook at KR2 went to QB2, there the move is written: R(KR2)-QB2.

The Forsythe Notation

This is used for copying out a position without having to use a diagram to indicate the placing of the various pieces and Pawns. In writing out the notation the player always reads it from White's side of the board, beginning with the top left hand corner (a8) and reading left to right, coming down the board rank by rank and ending with n1.

The notation, rank by rank, indicates the piece, and the blank square by using the initial letter of the pieces, and figures for the blank squares. The White pieces are indicated by Capital letters and the Black pieces by small letters.

For example, the following position occurred after the 23rd move in the 10th Match game between Petrosian and Spassky in 1966:

r2q1rk1/7p/p2p4/nppP4/2P2nB1/1P2n3/PQ1N3P/5RK1

This would mean that on White's eighth rank there is a Black Rook on the first square, the next two squares are blank, then Black Queen, one blank square, Black Rook, Black King and one blank square. In the same way the position on every rank is shown. Capital letters indicate White pieces.

It must be borne in mind that the Forsythe notation is always written while reading the board from White's side only. Players will find this system useful for noting the adjournment positions on the sealing envelopes, quickly noting a position from a book, etc.

Abbreviations used in Notations: Although these have been explained in the foregoing pages, they are being noted down now for the sake of continuity and explaining all about notation at one place.

0-0	= Castles with the Rook h1 or h8 (King side)
0-0-0	= Castles with the Rook a1 or a8 (Queen side)
=	= Promotion
× or :	= Takes (Capture)
+ or ch	= Check
‡	= Mate
!	= Well played
?	= Bad move.

VII

PLANNING, METHOD AND THE TIME FACTOR

It is much more important to look around than to look ahead. You must remember that more games are lost by overlooking the obvious than by failure to see far ahead.

Nevertheless, Chess players must always think ahead at least one move. That is, they must never move without first making sure that opponents cannot surprise them with a combination. It is for this reason the principle MOBILITY IS PARAMOUNT is repeatedly asserted. However, a player usually thinks further than one move. After development of the game is completed and your pieces are all in play, you should begin to look for a feasible objective.

For example, in some positions you may decide that an attack on your opponent's King is justified. In others, you may decide that such a plan is likely to fail and is therefore bad. But you may find you can win some material, perhaps a Pawn.

More often than not you would find that it is necessary to be less ambitious. Then a good recipe is to look for your piece that is doing least in the position, or one that is doing very little. Then make a plan to activate it. Or look for the enemy Piece that is most effective, or one that is very effective. Then make a plan to reduce its force, either by exchanging it or inducing its retreat. Try both the methods over in your mind.

Whatever plan you adopt, be ever ready to change it. A plan is only something to guide you while the position retains all the characteristics that led you to form the plan in the first place.

Above all, a plan must always take second place to immediate threats—either threats by your opponent or opportunities for strong threats of your own. Threats are the stuff of which combinations are made and combinations always have precedence over plans. Plans are what you fall back on when there is no sound combination. Admittedly that happens most of the time.

Method

High chess skill needs imagination and intuition. But you will develop these qualities all the sooner by thinking methodically, and you would avoid many blunders. Here is the guidelines called the Purdy Method. Follow it at every move.

(a) What are the opponent's threats? Or objects? The threats must be known, but before parrying them, see if they can be ignored.

(b) Have I a sound combination? (See the chapter mobility: combinations).

(c) If not, what should be my aims?

(d) Before playing any move, consider: Will this allow my opponent a sound combination?

(e) During your opponent's turn to move: make a reconnaissance, eyeing quickly all the squares each unit on the board commands. How safe are the Kings? And other Pieces? What Pawns are weak? What squares?

Always keep asking these questions to yourself. Be always alert for a little carelessness in chess might make you lose the game. A cool, collected and calculative brain is what a chess player must have.

The Time Factor: Try to get the most out of each move. Therefore prefer to bring fresh force into play rather than move a piece that is already in play. This principle applies right through the game. The player who completes the development first has the initiative, which is a real advantage. Apart from positions in which no progress possible, a player who makes a non-progressive move is said to 'lose a move', or in chess parlance, 'lose a tempo'.

The loss of a tempo may be of little importance or it may make all the difference between winning and losing. In other words, a tempo has no constant value.

However, it can be given a material value in the opening because in the opening the general objective is always the same—rapid development of the seven fighting pieces (omitting the King). At this stage a tempo is usually worth nearly half a Pawn. Knowing this helps you to decide whether to take an offered Pawn.

In case you win a Pawn in the opening but lose three tempos (or tempi) in doing so (e.g., by having to move an already developed piece three times) your opponent, attacking chances should outweigh your small material gain, as a rule. If you happen to be playing Black, so much the worse, because Black can be reckoned as beginning the game already half a tempo behind because White moves first. If, when the Pawn is offered, White is still his half-tempo ahead, Black will come out 3½ tempi behind.

But if White wins a Pawn at the same cost, White comes out only 2-1/2 tempi behind, and could consider taking the Pawn unless the position is very open i.e. several Pawns have already been exchanged. For in open positions a lead in tempi (development) tells more than in closed ones (very cluttered with Pawns).

An apt example to illustrate gain and loss of tempi is the opening: 1. e2-e4 e7-e5; 2. Ng1-f3 Nb8-e6; 3. d2-d4 (known as the Scotch game). Now Black will naturally play 3, ... e5×d4. If White recaptures with 4. Nf3×d4, that also will be a non-developing move because the White Knight was already developed. So neither side loses a tempo.

Alternatively, White may play 4 Bf1-c4 known as the Scotch Gambit (a gambit is a small sacrifice of material, usually a Pawn for gain in position). If then Black protects its Pawn with the developing move 4. ....Bf8-c5, White has yielded a Pawn for a bargain, but here the move, 5. c2-c3!, while not in itself a developing move, makes sure of opening up the position if Black is to retain its Pawn. Plus, as experience shows that White's compensation for the Pawn is about enough.

Now suppose White quietly recaptures, 4. Nf3×d4. Here a frequent error is 4. ... Nc6×d4.

Remember that AN EXCHANGE OF A DEVELOPED PIECE FOR A DEVELOPED PIECE ALWAYS LOSES A TEMPO FOR THE PLAYER WHO INITIATED THE SWAP, IF THE OPPONENT RECAPTURES WITH A DEVELOPING MOVE.

This is easily proved: A has reduced the number of developed pieces on side by one (since both pieces end up in the box), and if B, recaptures with a developing move the latter is clearly one up.

After 5. Qd1×d4 Black could ingeniously try 5...Qd8-f6, hoping White will either move its Queen (non-developing move) or else swap Queens, giving back the tempo by the rule in 'bold' print above. But White need do neither. Simply 6. Bc1-e3 is a developing move. If then Black exchanges Queens, it is true that this time he does not lose a tempo, as White will recapture with an already moved piece, indeed, neither side gains a tempo and White stays 1-1/2 tempi ahead. You might think White would gain a tempo with 6. e4-e5, forcing Black's Queen to move again. But no, e4-e5 is not a developing move, since it does not open a line for any un-developed White piece, as 1. e2-e4 did.

In this connection, another typical position of the Pieces deserves especial mention. That is called the 'Zugzwang'. It means you are forced to move to lose your positional or material advantage. It can be defined as a blockade position in which any move is disadvantageous to the blockaded player. Exceptionally, a tempo may have a minus value, for there are end-game positions in which having the move is fatal. This is the position of Zugzwang, a German word, meaning move-compulsion. Many end-games feature this motif.

VIII

THE END-GAME TECHNIQUES

The end game play is perhaps the most engrossing part of a chess game. This is the decisive phase of the game where the crown himself comes out to defend his own self. In the last stages most of the material has been removed from the board and the situation looks somewhat less confusing with each piece having quite open files and ranks. Although the situation here may appear quite uncomplicated yet the very simplicity of the end-game adds in practice to its difficulty and lends it an aura of mystery. Howsoever good a player be, his true strength and ability can be reliably judged from this final phase of the game. In this phase the moves played by the masters are easily distinguishable for they play with the total count of moves counted and re-counted in their brains. It is for this reason that invariably all masters are believed to be the maestros of this phase.

But, may one ask, what is the point to reckon the beginning of the end-game and the end-game of the middle-game when scores of times even a few moves after the beginning end the game in toto? Barring a few exceptions, normally the end-game starts when the game has just a few more moves left. At the final stage the player is usually confronted by one of the tasks to exploit the advantage he has gained in the earlier part of the game and convert it into a win or neutralise his opponent's advantage by accurate defence and draw the game. Of course, if he has failed to gain an advantage in the middle game, he can try to obtain it here.

The beginning of the end-game is usually reckoned when there is a relatively small number of pieces left on the board, and, but for the rare exceptions, direct attacks on the King with complications typical of the middle game are possible. The concluding stage of a game of chess has its characteristic peculiarities which, in comparison with the middle game, alter the whole approach to the position and the significance of the forces in action on the board.

It is also the 'royal' part of the game because it's involves a lot of king's activity. Having "sat out" the whole game behind the Pawn bastions in its own camp, the king now becomes an active piece and tries to participate in the struggle with all its might. It falls upon the opponent's prices and forges its way to the enemy camp in a chivalrous mood!

Despite the comparatively less number of pieces that are left on the board, each piece now has its enhanced value. For success it is important to know how to organise the cooperation of the pieces among themselves and with the pawns.

At times you would find the lack of forces at your command in this stage of the game. Hence it is all the more necessary to use your pieces judiciously and intelligently. In order to obtain a sufficient material superiority one must try to promote the Pawns as much as possible. This means that since every "insignificant" Pawn may, given a chance, become a mighty piece—a Queen or Rook for instance—

with their value is on the threshold of a tremendous increase. Pawn promotion is one of the most needed strategy at this stage of the game.

In short, for your convenience, we are giving the brief guidelines for the good play at this stage.

End-game Hints

(i) As you have now few pieces, see that you make the most of each one. For this purpose try to avoid having to use a piece for a delusive task, especially a Rook. It is only when aggressively posted that a piece pulls its full weight.

(ii) Remember that in the end-game the King is a fighting piece. Make use of it.

(iii) A Rook's goal is the seventh rank. Here it attacks Pawns which cannot possibly call other Pawns to their support. A Rook here is particularly strong if at the same time it confines the enemy King to his back rank.

(iv) If you have a Bishop, whether the enemy has one or not, place your Pawns on the opposite colour to that occupied by your own Bishop.

To beginners this rule for Bishop and Pawns sound silly, because it deprives the Pawn of the Bishop's support. However, on opposite colours the Bishop and Pawns together command more squares; they do not overlap. It is the same reasons that makes two Bishops so strong.

(v) Always remember the Passed Pawn is the soul of the end-game. A Passed Pawn advanced to the sixth or seventh rank is often worth a piece.

(vi) With an advantage, keep Pawns on both wings. This helps to avoid a draw. If there are Pawns on one wing only, the advantage of one Pawn extra is, more often than not, in sufficient to win.

Hence remember the Old Rule: for winning, exchange Pieces; for drawing, exchange Pawns.

SOME SIMPLE CHECKMATES POSITIONS

Rook and Knight

1 Ne4–f6 + Kg8–h8
2 Rf7–h7#

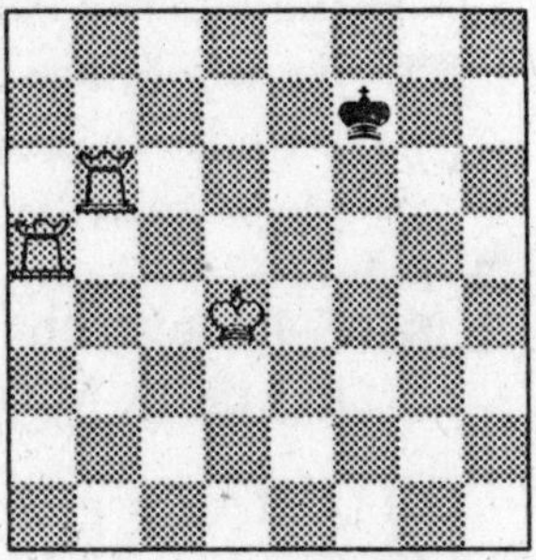

Two Rooks

1 Ra5–a7+ Kf7–e8, f8 or g8
2 Rb6–b8#

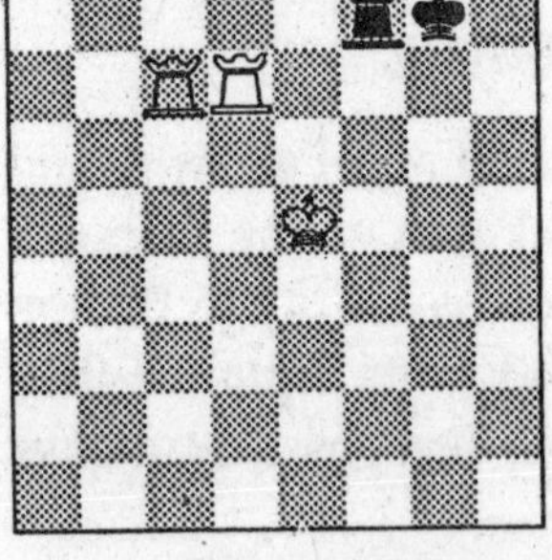

Two Rooks

1 Rd7–g7+ Kg8–h8
2 Rg7–h7+ Kh8–g8
3 Rc7–g7#

Back row (or rank)

1 Rd5–d8+ Rc8×d8
2 Rd4×d8#

Rook and Bishop

1 Re1–g1+ Kg8–h8
2 Bc3×f6#

Queen and Knight

1 Qb5–d7+ Kc8–b8
2 Ne5–c6+ kb8–a8
3 Qd7–a7 or c8#

Queen and Bishop

1 Qb4–e7 Kc8–b8
2 Qe7–b7#

Queen and King

1 Qg4–g7+ Ke7–d8
2 Ke5–d6 kd8–c8
3 Qg7–c7#
Or if 2 ... Kd8–e8;
3 ... Qg7–e7#

The above shown eight checkmates reveal how Pieces work together forcing checkmates.

In case only the enemy King is left on the board, you need at least the following forces to achieve checkmates:

(i) King and Queen;

(ii) King and Rook;

(iii) King and two Bishops;

(iv) King, Knight and Bishop; and

(v) King and two Bishops and a Knight or two Knights and a Bishop and (in case you are able to promote your Pawn) three Knights.

At times when the enemy Pieces are blocking the movement of their own King, it may be possible to checkmates with less material—even with a Pawn supported by another Piece.

However, you cannot force checkmate against a lone King with only a King and Bishop or even with a King and two Knights. Such endings are therefore drawn. Similarly King versus King is drawn! You might think that it is unnecessary but at times the novice chase the enemy King all over the board in a vain pursuit.

The above mentioned checkmates positions are shown to make you memorise them because when you reach this position you need not devise new moves. Just apply the set formula and the game is yours!

The Set Patterns of Checkmates

Each of the four diagrams below has been divided into four parts for convenience. Thus each of the divided diagrams represents a set pattern. In all there are 32 patterns.

1. Queen Checkmates

(1) Queen with King support

(2) Queen with King support

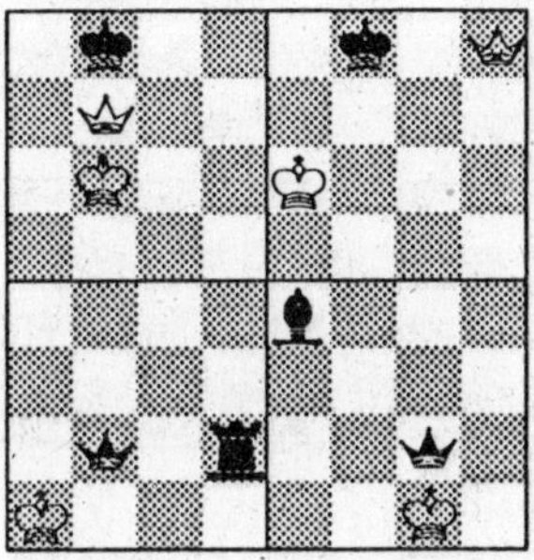

(3) Queen with Rook

(4) Queen with Bishop

(5) Queen with Knight

(6) Queen with Pawn

(7) Queen aided by enemy Pawn occupying escape square

(8) Queen aided by two enemy pieces occupying escape squares

2. Rook Checkmates

(9) Rook with King

(10) Two Rooks

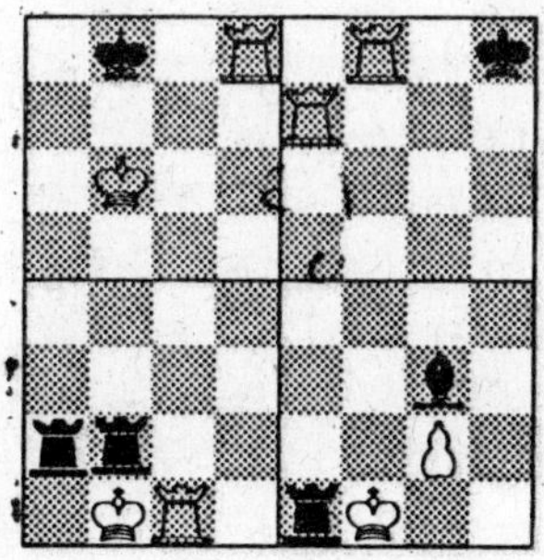

(11) Two Rooks

(12) Rook and Bishop

(13) Rook and Knight

(14) Rook and Pawn

(15) Rook (back row mate)

(16) Rook and Knight

3. Bishop Checkmates

(17) Bishop mate with King's escape square blocked by its own pieces

(18) Two Bishops co-operating with their King

(19) Two Bishops with escape square occupied by enemy Pawn

(20) Two Bishops mating with 'scissors' pattern

(21) Bishop aided by Knight

(22) Similar to (21) but with the Knight covering escape square from a different position

(23) Bishop aided by Rook

(24) Bishop mate with support by Knight and Bishop

4. Knight Checkmates

(25) Knight mates aided by King

(26) Knight mates with Pawn help

(27) Knight in the amusing 'smothered-mate' position

(28) Two Knights trap the enemy King

(29) Knight mates with Bishop support

(30) Knight and Bishop in a different mating pattern

(31) Knight and Rook mate

(32) Knight mates with Queen help

SOME SPECIAL END-GAME ILLUSTRATION

1. King and Pawn *v* King

(a) *A Simple Technique*

The smallest material advantage you can have is one Pawn more than your opponent. If this is reduced in the end-game to a contest of King and Pawn *v* King, the chances of winning depend on whether the Pawn can be promoted.

In the diagram ahead the winning method is made quite clear:

(i) White to play
(ii) Black to play

(i) With White to move, the player with the Pawn wins by

1 d7–d8 = Q or R#

(ii) With Black to move, the win is also quite simple to bring about.

1 . . .	Kb8–a8
2 d7–d8 = Q or R#	

In the next diagram below the problem of promoting the Pawn requires a little more thought. Firstly the white King must gain control of the queening square c8.

(i) White to play
(ii) Black to play

(i) With White to move the following method wins:

1 Kc6–d6	Kc8–d8
2 c5–c6	Kd8–c8
3 c6–c7	Kc8–b7
4 Kd6–d7	K moves
5 c7–c8 = Q	

and wins

(ii) With Black to move the method is even more simple:

1 ... Kc8–d8; 2 Kc6–b7! The white King now controls all the squares on the Pawn's route to the queening square, i.e., c6, c7 and c8. 2 ... Kd8–d7; 3 c5–c6+, kd7–d8; 4 c6–c7+, Kd8–d7; 5 c7–c8=Q+ and wins.

Similarly after 1 ... Kc8–b8; 2 Kc6–d7, Kb8–b7; 3 c5–c6+, Kb7–b8; 4 c6–c7+, Kb8–b7; 5 c7–c8 = Q+and wins.

(b) *The Special Case of the Rook's Pawn*

An interesting fact is that a Rook's Pawn cannot be promoted if the defending King occupies the queening square. A Rook's Pawn is one on either file a or h.

Black to play

Thus in this diagram after:

1 ...	Ka8–b8
2 Ka6–b6	Kb8–a8
3 a5–a6	Ka8–b8
4 a6–a7	Kb8–a8
5 Kb6–a6	

Stalemate! Draw

or

5 Kb6–a5, b5 or c6	Kb8×a7 and draws

A similar result arises if White plays first.

In the position in the diagram below the draw is arrived at by preventing the White King from clearing file a for the Pawn's path.

Thus after:

1 Ka8–a7	Kc8–c7
2 Ka7–a8	Kc7–c8, etc.

or

1 a6–a7	Kc8–c7! Stalemate

Similar results are brought about with Black to move first.

(c) *Learning to Count*

The position in the diagram below illustrates a frequent end-game situation, where the problem of promoting the Pawn is a matter of counting the number of moves to the queening square. In such a situation there are a number of reliable ways of deciding if a Pawn may queen safely, and the following method is recommended.

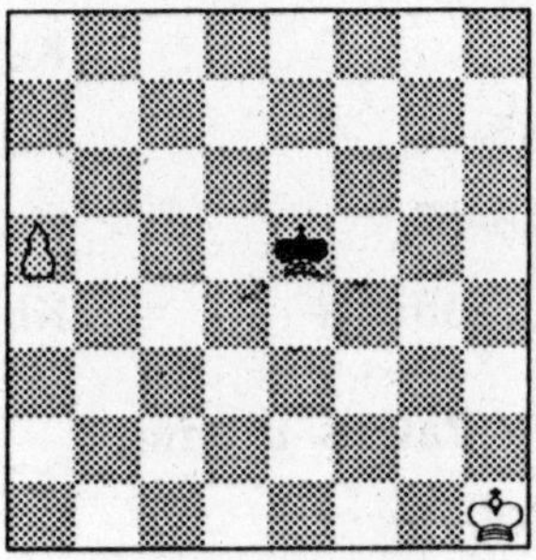

(i) White to play
(ii) Black to play

The Pawn may reach the queening square a8 in three moves: a6, a7 and a8. The black King would take four moves, e.g. one possible route would be: d6, c7, b7 and a8.

(i) Thus after White plays:

1 a5–a6	Ke5–d6
2 a6–a7	Kd6–c7
3 a7–a8 = Q	

The black King would still be on c7.

From such a series of moves, and with no other pieces concerned, the following counting method can be suggested:

With a Pawn to move, it queens safely if it succeeds in reaching the queening square in fewer moves than the opposing King.

(ii) Now consider the same position in the diagram above, but with Black to move. After 1 ... Ke5–d6 it would be the Pawn's turn to move, and now the rule applies as before. The Pawn still needs only three moves to reach the queening square, but the black King only three moves as well.

Since the Pawn is not able to queen in fewer moves it is lost.

1 ...	Ke5–d6
2 a5–a6	Kd6–c7
3 a6–a7	Kc7–b7
4 a7–a8=Q+	Kb7×a8

2. King and Two Pawns *v* King

(a) *Widely Separated Pawns*

In the diagram below a position is shown in which White wins because the black King cannot divide its attention successfully between the two white Pawns. Black would draw if there was no white Pawn on e4. Check this with the counting method.

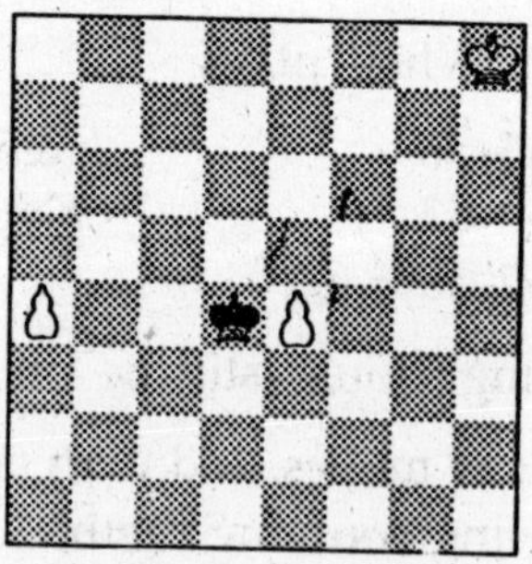

White to play

However, in the position shown White wins by:

1 a4–a5	Kd4×e4

and the white Pawn requires a further three moves to queen, while the black King needs four moves to reach a8. The counting method confirms that the Pawn queens safely.

Alternatively, Black may try a different defence.

1 a4–a5	Kd4–c5
2 a5–a6	Kc5–b6
3 e4–e5!	Kb6×a6

In which case the Pawn on e5 queens without being captured. By the counting method the Pawn has three moves from e5 to e8, whilst the black King on square a6 requires four moves, and thus fails to stop the Pawn.

Note that after 1 a4–a5, Kd4–c5; 2 a5–a6, Kc5–b6 White would make a mistake to play 3 a6–a7? for after 3 ... Kb6×a7 the remaining Pawn is now only on square e4, and requires four moves to queen. The opposing King captures it in the same number of moves.

The key move then was 3 e4–e5 which stretched the black King's attention beyond the limit.

What is White's winning method in position in the diagram below?

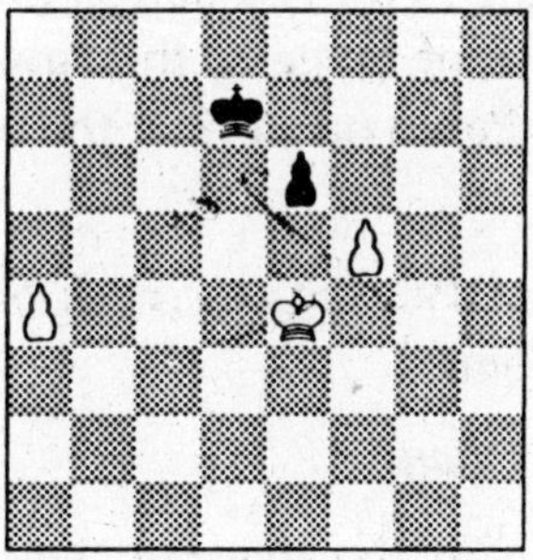

White to play

If

1 a4–a5	e6×f5+

2 Ke4×f5	Kd7–c7
3 a5–a6	Kc7–b6

And Black draws.

Similarly Black draws if:

1 Ke4-e5	e6×f5
2 a4–a5	Kd7–c7, etc.

Also if

1 f5×e6+	Kd7×e6
2 a4–a5 or	

Ke4–d4

And Black has time to move his King across to a8, reaching a drawn position similar to earlier diagram.

White's winning method is to rely on a similar situation to that shown in the previous example—diagram and to play:

1 f5–f6!

Black is now unable to attend to both queening threats from the white Pawns on a4 and f6.

If the black King is moved across to capture the Pawn on file f, he goes out of range of the Pawn on a4. Similarly if he attends to the Pawn on a4 first, the other Pawn queens safely.

Widely separated Pawns can stretch the defending King's efforts beyond the limit.

(b) *Self-Supporting Pawns*

In the position in the diagram below the two white Pawns appear to be at the mercy of the black King. Yet if the Pawns stand firm, and wait for the white King to move across, at least one of the Pawns will queen.

For if

1 ... Ke6×e5?

This allows White's other Pawn to escape to the queening square.

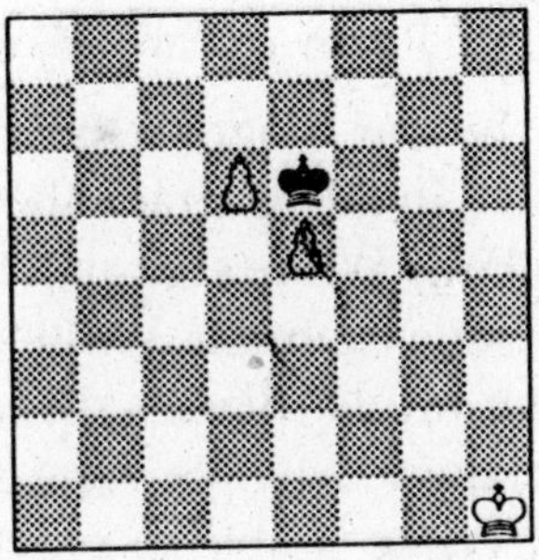

2 d6–d7 Ke5–e6

3 d7–d8 = Q

Black may instead just remain on guard moving backwards and forwards on d7 and e6. In this case White will brings his King across in order to shepherd the Pawns to the 8th rank.

For example, in the along side diagram the white King has reached the Pawns.

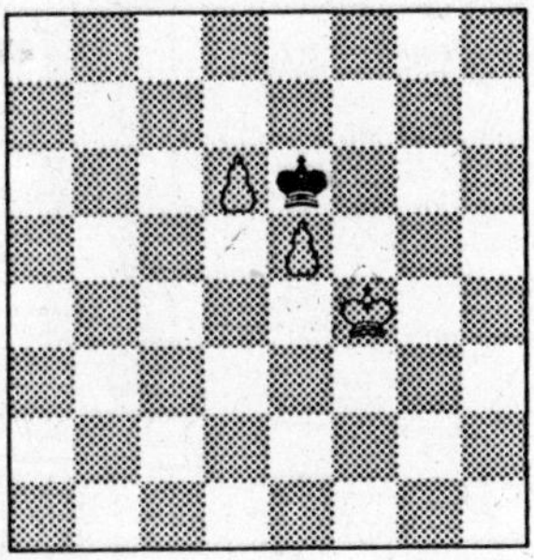

1 Kf4–g5 Ke6–d7

2 Kg5–f6

And now the black King has no adequate defence. One possible winning variation for White would be:

2 ... Kd7–e8

3 e5–e6 Ke8–d8

4 Kf6–f7 Kd8–c8

5 e6–e7

And queens next move.

When two Pawns are on neighbouring files, one supporting the other, the supporting Pawn cannot be captured safely by the enemy King.

3. King and Two Pawns *v* King and Pawn

(a) *With One of the Two Pawns a 'Passed' Pawn*

You will remember that a passed Pawn is one which on route to its queening square is not blocked by an enemy Pawn on its file, nor has to cross a square attacked by an enemy Pawn on an adjoining file.

In the diagram below is a similar position to that shown in the diagram above but with Black having a Pawn blocking White's supporting Pawn. As illustrated in the previous example, White's strength lies in this supporting Pawn on d4. Black's difficulty is that he can only defend his Pawn with his King from two squares—c6 and e6—and White is able to prevent him from using these defensive squares.

(i) White to play
(ii) Black to play

(i) With White to move, Black has no time to occupy e6, and can only defend his Pawn from c6. White's task is quite straightforward.

1 Ke3–f4	Kc6–d7
2 Kf4–e5	

Attacking Black's Pawn.

2 ...	Kd7–c6
3 Ke5–e6	

Still attacking the Pawn, and now Black's King has to move away from its defence.

After

3 ...	Kc6–c7 or b7
4 Ke6×d5	

And White should have no difficulty in promoting one of his Pawns.

(ii) In the diagram above with Black to move, the winning method is a little longer, as in this case Black has time to occupy square e6 with his King. For the time being this denies White entry on to this square.

1 ...	Kc6–d7
2 Ke3–f4	Kd7–e6

But White can force Black's King away:

3 Kf4–g5!	Ke6–e7
4 Kg5–f5	Ke7–d7
5 Kf5–e5	Kd7–c6

The same position as that reached in (i) above

6 Ke5–e6

And White wins as before.

(b) *With Neither Pawn Passed*

In the position in the diagram below, White's extra Pawn is not a passed Pawn. White has to play most carefully to avoid a draw.

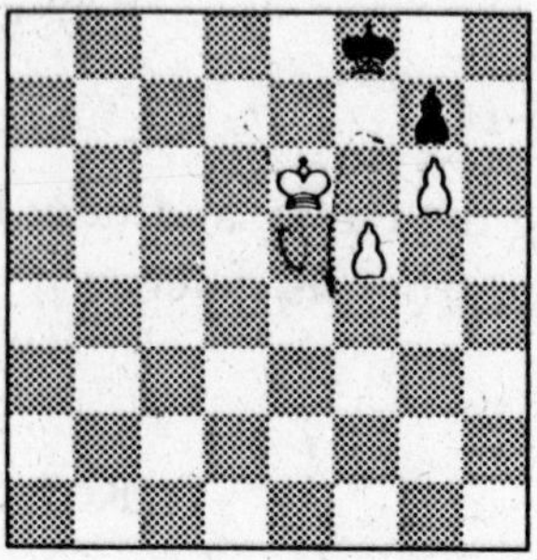

White to play

Here are three of these drawing possibilities:

(i) If

1 f5–f6	Kf8–g8
2 f6×g7	Kg8×g7
3 Ke6–f5	

To defend the remaining Pawn. But Black has the opposition, and with White's King not in front of his Pawn a draw results.

3 ...	Kg7–g8
4 Kf5–f6	Kg8–f8
5 g6–g7+	Kf8–g8

And next move White must give stalemate by 6 Kf6–g6, or give up his Pawn.

(ii) If

1 f5–f6	Kf8–g8

And then

2 Ke6–e7	g7×f6
3 Ke7×f6	Kg8–f8

Reaching the same position as that after Black's 4th move in variation (i) above. Thus Black manages to draw.

(iii) If

1 f5–f6 Kf8–g8

And then

2 f6–f7+ Kg8–f8

3 Ke6–d6 or d7

gives stalemate, and White's only other choice is to move back to rank 5 on to square d5, e5 or f5. This allows Black to move out with ... Kf8–e7, and draw by moving back and forth from e7 to f8.

Black must not reply to 1 f5–f6 with 1 ... g7×g6; for 2 Ke6×f6, Kf8–g8; 3 g6–g7, Kg8–h7; 4 Kf6–f7 and wins.

White's winning method requires three steps, to be achieved, in the following order:

Step 1– Move the white King to a square ready to occupy square f7.

Step 2– Dislodge Black's blocking Pawn with the move f5–f6.

Step 3– Occupy square f7 with the white King.

White is then in a position to escort his remaining Pawn home to its queening square, with mate to follow.

Here are the moves—starting from the diagram above:

1 Ke6–d7	Kf8–g8
2 Kd7–e7	Kg8–h8

Step 1 achieved. Not too hasty here though, for 3 Ke7–f7 stalemates the black King.

3 f5–f6	g7×f6

Step 2 achieved. For if instead 3 ... Kh8–g8; 4 f6–f7+, Kg8–h8; 5 f7–f8 = Q#!

4 Ke7–f7

Step 3 completes the winning method. Although the alternative 4 Ke7×f6 also wins, the variation that follows is quicker, and therefore more efficient.

4 ...	f6–f5
5 g6–g7+	Kh8–h7
6 g7–g8 = Q+	Kh7–h6
7 Qg8–g6 =	

4. Rook and Pawn *v* Rook

(a) *With Supporting Rook behind the Pawn*

Diagram below illustrates the best situation for shepherding a passed Pawn—with a supporting Rook behind it. The Pawn may safely advance to its queening square.

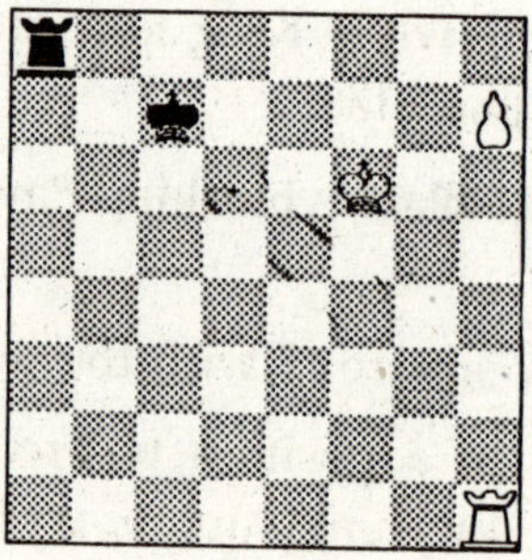

White to play

1 h7–h8 = Q	Ra8×h8
2 Rh1×h8	

And an easy win for White; King and Rook *v* King.

The position illustrated in the diagram ahead is slightly more difficult, showing a black Rook blocking the way of the Pawn. By attacking the black Rook with the white King, and driving it away, the Pawn will queen.

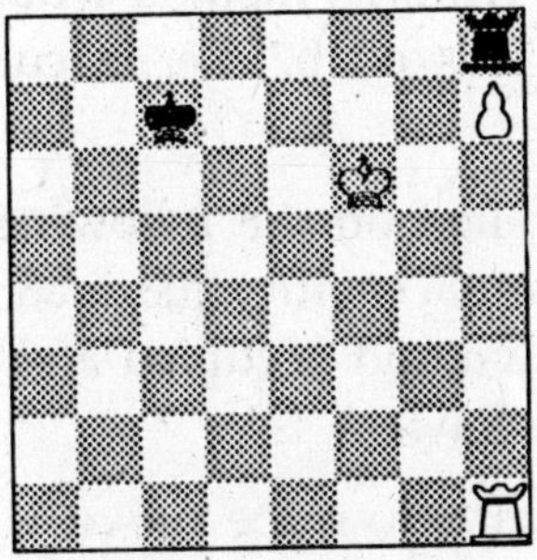

White to play

1 Kf6–g7	Rh8–a8
2 h7–h8 = Q	

And a simple win follows.

(b) *With Supporting Rook in Front of the Pawn*

Diagram below, illustrates another situation, but with supporting Rook in front of the Pawn. To move the white Rook away would allow Black to capture the Pawn with his Rook.

But White has a neat idea!

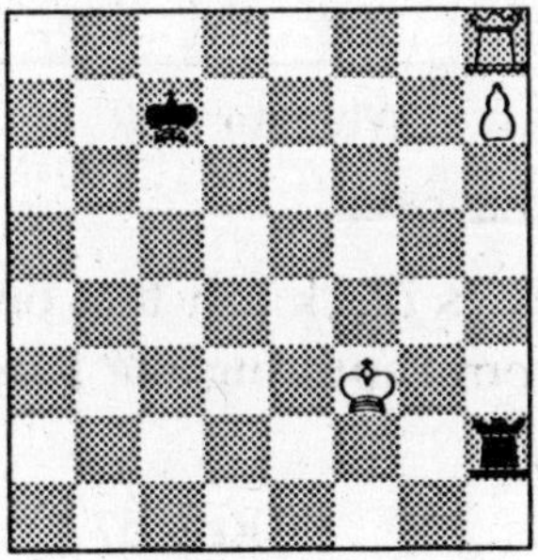

White to play

For after:

1 Rh8–a8!	Rh2×h7
2 Ra8–a7+	Kc7–b6
3 Ra7×h7	
And wins!	

Note that this winning method would not be possible if the black King was on b7, i.e. in contact with square a8.

The method relied on the following facts—the black King was not in contact with square a8, it was separated from the white Pawn and occupied a square on the same rank as the white Pawn.

But in diagram below the move 1 Rh8–a8 does not work, for after 1 ... Rh2×h7 there is no check of the black King, compelling it to move and exposing the black Rook to capture.

Yet there is another winning method for white.

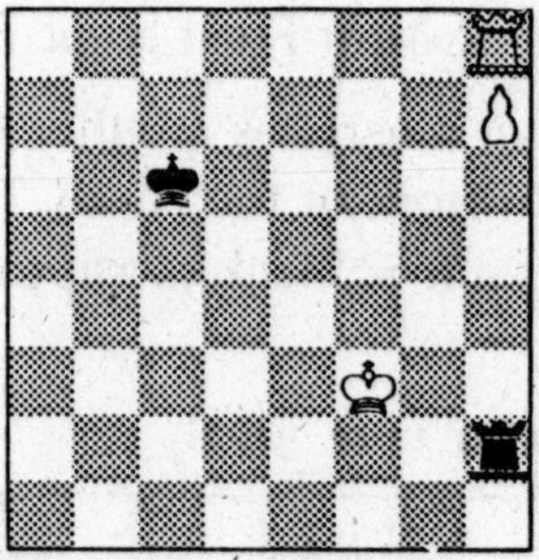

White to play

1 Rh8–c8+!

The check delays Black just that one move necessary to prevent him from capturing the Pawn with his Rook. Thus after:

1 ...	Kc6–d7
2 h7–h8 = Q	

And after 2 ... Rh2×h8; 3 Rc8×h8, White wins easily.

There are very many different situations with Rooks and Pawns in the end-game, requiring a special plan to deal with each one of them. As your experience grows you will able to examine and understood more difficult positions.

5. Bishop and Pawn *v* Bishop

(a) *With the Defending King In front of the Pawn*

Diagram below illustrates the ideal situation for the defending side to bring about a draw. The defending black King is occupying a square of opposite colour to that used by the opposing Bishop, and also this King stands in front of the Pawn.

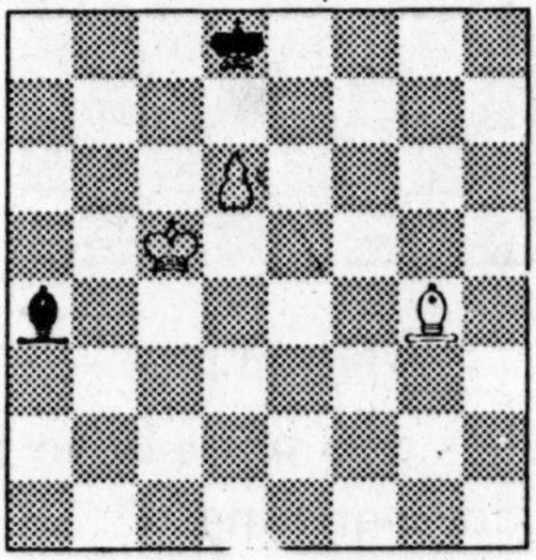

White to play

Thus the white Bishop, operating solely on white squares, is unable to give check to the defending King. All that Black needs to do is move his Bishop to a safe square each move, leaving his King on d8, from which it cannot be shifted.

For example:

1 Bg4–f5	Ba4–b3
2 Kc5–b6	Bb3–c4 or d5

And so on! Black draws.

(b) *With the Defending King Unable To Occupy A Square in front of the Pawn*

In the diagram below it is clear the black King has no chance of occupying square d8 in front of the white

Pawn. However, playing 1 d6–d7 does not win for White, because Black can always give up his Bishop for the Pawn and draw. King and Bishop is not a sufficient force with which to mate a lone King. Thus Black could reply 1 ... Ba4×d7 and draw.

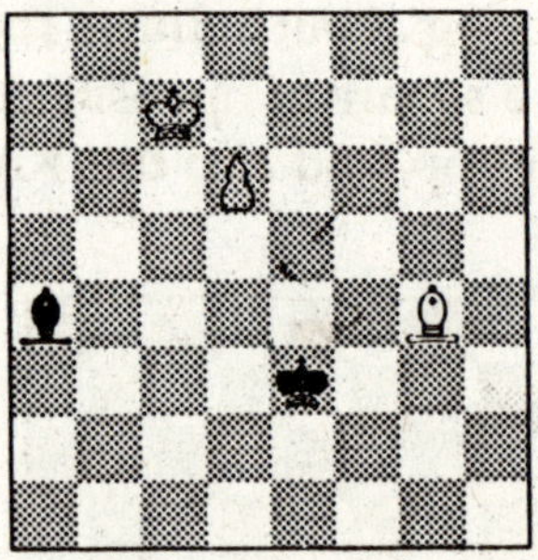

White to play

Therefore White's aim must be to prevent the black Bishop from attacking squaring d7.

Thus the move:

1 Bg4–d7

immediately compels Black to move his Bishop away, for 1 ... Ba4×d7; 2 Kc7×d7 loses for Black.

... Ba4–d1

Now White blocks his own Pawn's advance, and Black has placed his Bishop so that he retains the choice of two diagonals, both of which give control of square d7—either diagonal a4/e8 or h3/c8.

2 Bd7–c6

Compelling Black to cover d7 by

2 ... Bd1–g4

3 Bc6–b7!

Now Black must still retain his Bishop on diagonal h3/c8, because of the constant threat of White's Pawn advance d6–d7. For example:

3 ... Bg4–h3

4 Bb7–c8!

The white Bishop has found a safe square, other than in front of its own pawn, in order to drive the defending black Bishop away. Now Black cannot prevent d6–d7, and so White wins.

In the diagram below the difference here is that the white Bishop can occupy square f3, and from there immediately contest control of square d7 from c6 instead of c8, as in the previous example.

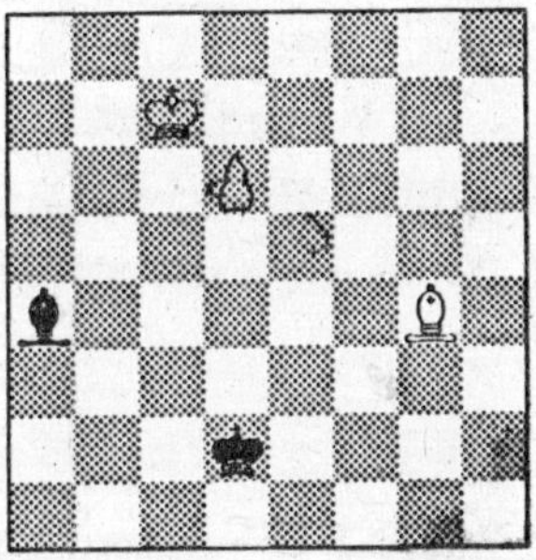

White to play

Thus play continues:

1 Bg4–f3 Ba4–b5 or e8

(or Black could make any King move)

2 Bf3–c6

And wins.

These are fairly simple ideas about Bishop endings. You will meet many different kinds as you go on playing.

6. Knight and Pawn *v* Knight

As in the examples of Bishop and Pawn *v* Bishop the defending side can always take any opportunity of giving up the minor piece for the Pawn.

Look at the diagram below. As King and Knight *v* King is not a mating force, then clearly 1 d7–d8 = Q is met by 1 ... Nf7×d8 and a draw results.

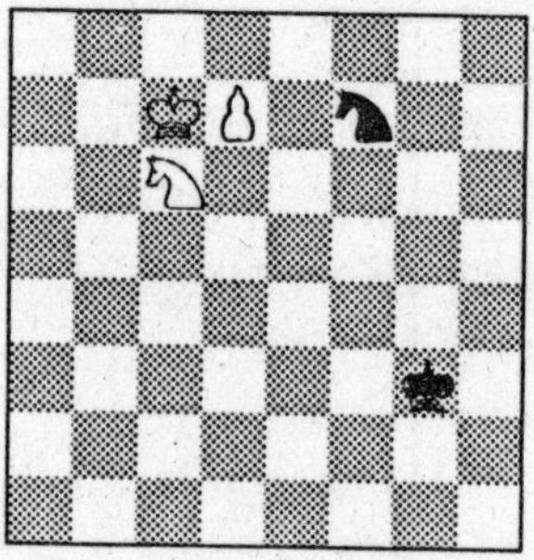

White to play

The black Knight controls the queening square from f7, and also has e6 as an alternative.

Thus after:

1 Nc6–e5!

Not 1 ... Nf7×e5?; 2 d7–d8 = Q and wins.

1 ... Nf7–g5

And now if 2 d7–d8=Q, Ng5–e6 +, forking King and Queen, achieving a draw.

But White wins by

2 Kc7–d6!

For now White prevents the black Knight from using e6 or f7.

2 ... Ng5–e4+

3 Kd6–c6 or e7

and wins, for whatever Black does, the Pawn queens safely.

7. Queen *v* Pawns

In the diagram below the white Queen is assisted by its King in attempting to capture the black Pawn, which has only the lone black King to protect it.

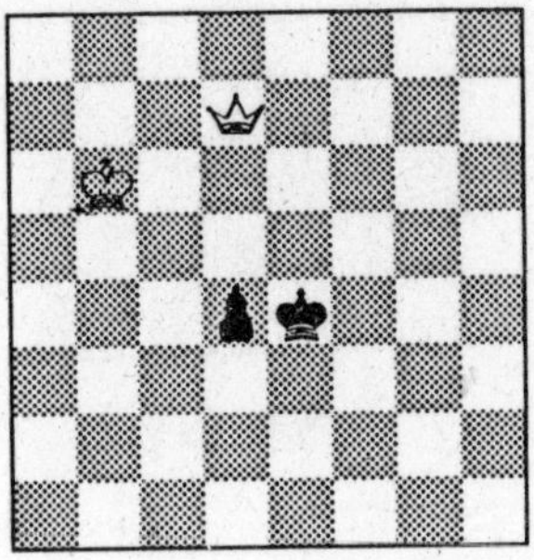

White to play

1 Kb6–c5

Threatening Qd7×d4+

1 ... d4–d3

2 Kc5–c4

A similar threat, but now the Pawn cannot advance without losing contact with the protecting black King.

2 ... Ke4–e3

3 Qd7×d3 +

And wins.

With the Pawn one move from its queening square and its King supporting it, there are possibilities of a draw. This is possible if the Pawn is on file a, c, f or h. But on all other files the side with the Queen should win.

The method for winning is to drive the supporting King on to the queening square, thus allowing time to move the attacking King towards the area, to assist the Queen.

The diagram below illustrates the method.

White to play

1 Qd4–e4+ Ke2–f2

2 Qe4–d3

Threatening to capture the Pawn

2 ... Kf2–e1

3 Qd3–e3+!

Forcing the black King in front of his Pawn, for if 3 ... Ke1–f1; 4 Qe3×d2.

3 ... Ke1–d1

4 Kb5–c4, Kd1–c2.

Black again prepares to queen the Pawn; 5 Qe3–c3+, Kc2–d1 or else the Pawn is lost; 6 Kc4–d3, Kd1–e1; 7 Qc3×d2+ and wins.

IX

SOME END-GAME FROM MASTERS' PLAY

Given below are some end-game situations that actually emerged in the celebrated players' contests. Our advice is that the young learners should try to play them independently only by looking at the diagrams and only when they feel confused or unable to find the right moves to finish the game that they should read the explanations given along to/below/above the diagrams. Then only they would learn the game better and detect the difference between theirs and Masters' play.

BOGNOR REGIS 1964

D.V. Mardle

D. Parr

Black to play

1 ...	Rf3–f4
Resigns	

Because if the white Rook moves away, then 2 ... Rf4×c4+ and the white Pawn on h4 is also lost.

Also if 2 Rg4×f4, e5×f4 and then the Pawn on h4 falls. The white King becomes tied down to preventing the passed Pawn on file from queening. White is compelled to make weakening moves with his Pawns, some of which will be captured.

Practice this position with an opponent to see what happens.

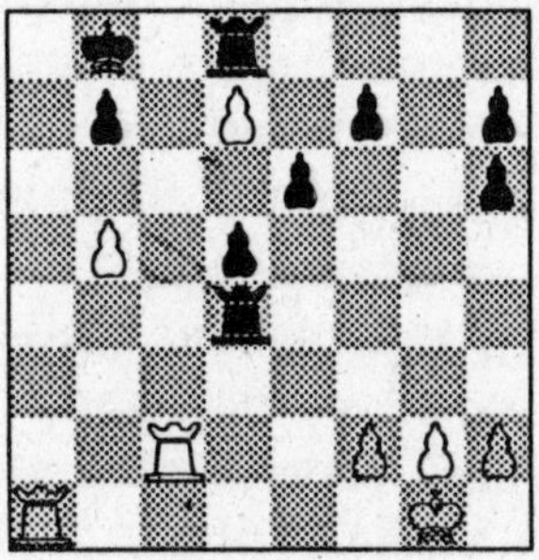

White to play

Possible continuation in position following resignation in Tal *v* Botwinnik, Moscow 1961 (8th game of World Championship match).

1 Rc2–c8+	Rd8×c8
2 Ra1–a8+ !	Kb8×a8
3 d7×c8 = Q+	Ka8–a7

And to add insult to injury!

4 Qc8–c5+

Forking King and Rook, and so the black Rook falls.

I. Zacharov

E. Geller
White to play

1 Nc4–e5!	Resigns

The power of a passed Pawn supported by a Rook behind it, is well shown here.

With this Knight move, White threatened 2 Ne5–d7, and to win material.

For example, the game may have continued:

1 ...	Bd8–c7
2 Ne5–d7	Rb8–d8
3 b7–b8 = Q	Bc7×b8
4 Rb3×b8	Rd8×b8
5 Nd7×b8	

A clear won ending for White, with the extra piece.

MOSCOW 1963

L. Szabo

P. Keres
White to play

1 Qa5–c3+	Qh7–g7
2 Re6×g6!	Resigns

For Black connot prevent both Queens and Rooks being exchanged and would then face no less than five Pawns with only a Bishop—a certain loss for Black.

The game may have continued:

2 ...	Qg7×c3
3 Rg6×g8+	Kh8×g8
4 b2×c3	

And White wins.

ENACHEDE 1963

J.M. Aitken

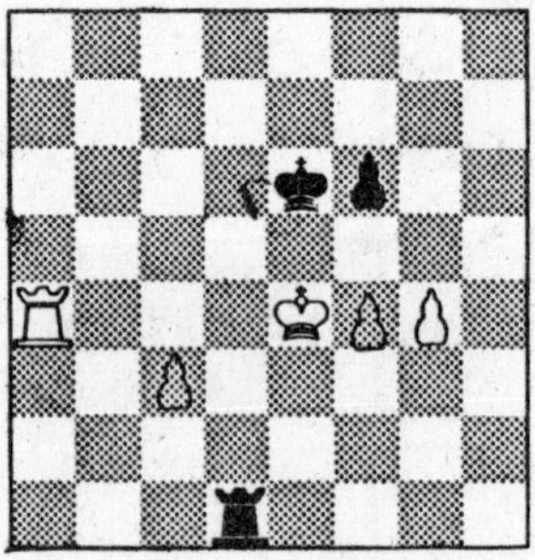

J. Penrose
White to play

1 Ra4–a6+	Ke6–e7
2 Ra6–c6	Resigns

For White must win the black Pawn on c5, and White's Pawn majority is enough to win.

MOSCOW 1964

D. Bronstein

A. Suetin

Black to play

1 ...	Nc2–e3!

Threatening ... g3–g2, and also preventing the white King advancing via c4.

2 Kc3–d3	g3–g2
3 Be4×g2	Ne3×g2
4 Kd3–e4	Kc7–d6

Black defends e5.

5 a3–a4	Ng2–f4

The Knight attacks h5.

6 a4–a5	b6×a5
7 b4×a5	Nf4×h5
8 a5–a6	Nh5–f6+
9 Ke4–f5	Nf6–d5
10 a6–a7	Nd5–b6
Resigns	

One of Black's Pawns would eventually queen. This ending illustrates further the power of the passed Pawn. White had to give up his Bishop, and Black's win was then just a matter of careful counting of moves.

ILFORD 1963

R. Persitz

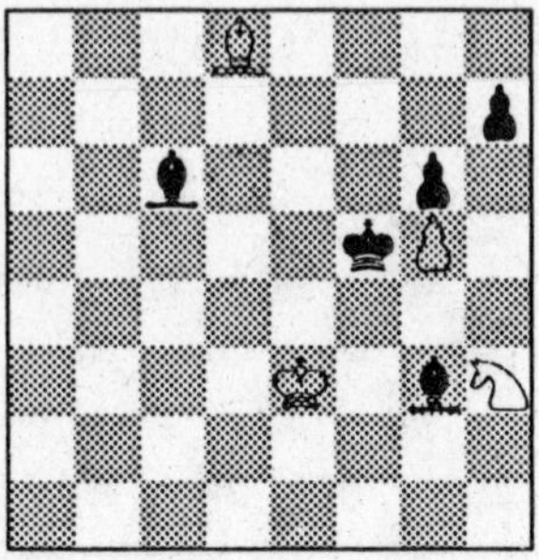

R.A. Fuller
Black to play

1 ...	Bc6–g2

Driving away one of White's pieces defending g5.

Resigns

White's position was hopeless. The game might have continued:

2 Nh3–f2	Bg3–h4
3 Nf2–d3	

There is no better move.

3 ...	Bh4×g5
4 Bd8×g5	Kf5×g5

And Black would win easily with the two Pawns.

ENSCHEDE 1963

L. Popov

J. Penrose
White to play

By a series of checks, Black's King has been forced out into an exposed position in the centre of the board.

1 Ra1–c1 +	Kc4–b3

If 1 ... Kc4–d3; 2 Re1–c3+. Kd3–d2; 3 Qe5–e3+, Kd2–d1; 4 Re3–c1#.

2 Qe5–c3+	Kb3–a2
3 b2–b4	Resigns

Black is faced with the mate threat 4 Rc1–a1!

PAIGNTON 1963

A.W. Bowen

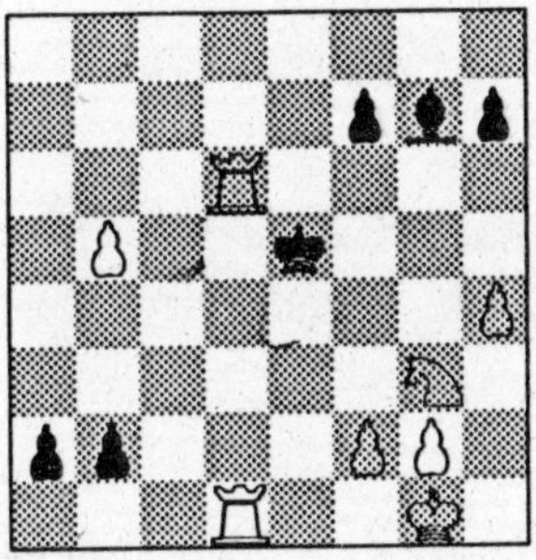

P.N. Wallis
White to play

Two black Pawns one move from queening, but White has trapped the black King in a mating net.

1 Rd1–d5+	Ke5–f4
2 Rd5–f5+	Kf4–g4
3 Kg1–h2!	Resigns

For if 3 ... b2–b1 = Q; 4 f2–f3+, Kg4×h4; and White follows up with Rf5–h5#.

Or if 3 ... Kg4×h4; 4 f2–f3, followed by Rf5–h5#.

BATH 1963

M.J. Franklin

O.M. Hindle
White to play

Saving an almost lost game by perpetual check!

1. Ne4×f6+	Kg8–f8; Not	1 ..., Kg8–h8;
2. Rd7–h7#		2. Re7–d7

Drawn—for Black has either the choice of useless checks with his Rook, or allowing the perpetual check.

For example:

2 ...	Rb2×b3
3 Nf6–h7+	Kf8–e8 or g8
4 Nh7–f6+	Ke8 or g8–f8

and so on.

Recapitulation of the Tactical Devices for Winning Material

We hope by now our young readers would be itching for the actual combat. Before doing so it is always better to memorise certain set patterns. These give you the material advantage and hence the aim of these tactical devices is to win material for you. Although they have been briefly explained in the foregoing pages under the

'Basics' chapter, their recapitulation with the illustrative diagrams is handy for better perception of the end-game play.

We all know that in battle the larger army is always the victor. However, there are times when a small army equipped with better weapons or resources scores over its apparently mightier adversary. The Mughal King, Babur's army could out manoeuvre Sultan Ibrahim Lodhi because of his better equipped artillery although his forces were much less than that of the Sultan. One good winning plan, therefore, is to try to reduce the size of your opponent's force by capturing his pieces without giving up so many of your own. This is what is called "Winning Material". For example, a common way of foreing a capture is by the use of 'double attack' or 'fork'. In double attack two or more pieces are attacked at the same time. If one of the two attacked pieces is made safe, the other may be captured.

Given below are some tactical devices most frequently used to win material.

BASIC PATTERNS

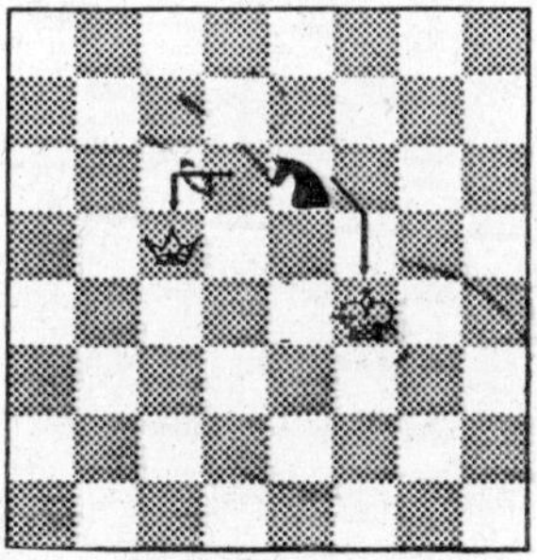

Knight Fork

Two or more pieces are attacked at the same time.

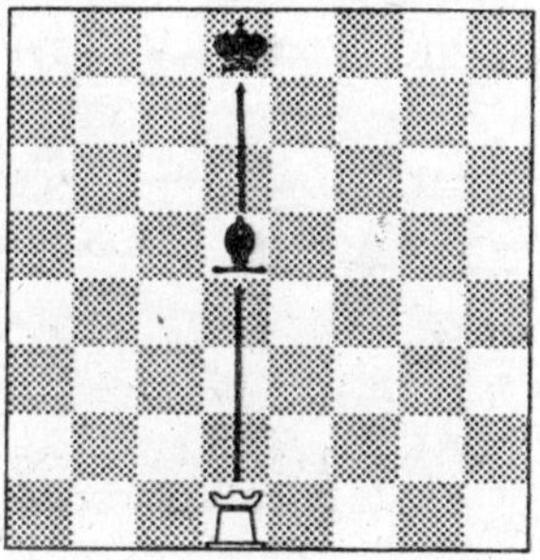

Pin

A piece is attacked on a line from which it cannot move without exposing another piece to attack, behind it.

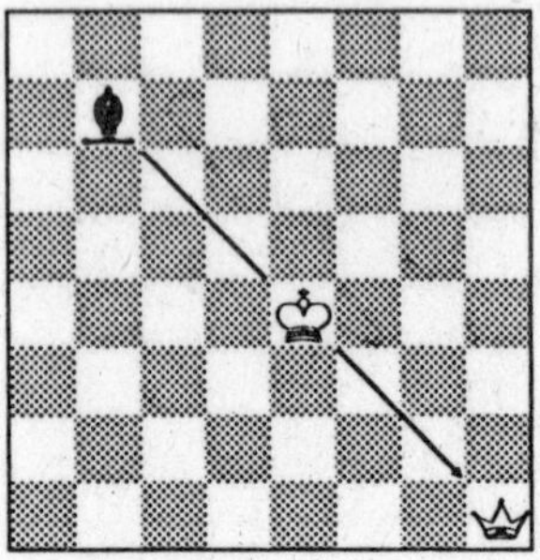

Skewer

An attack along a line where the piece nearer the attacker is compelled to move.

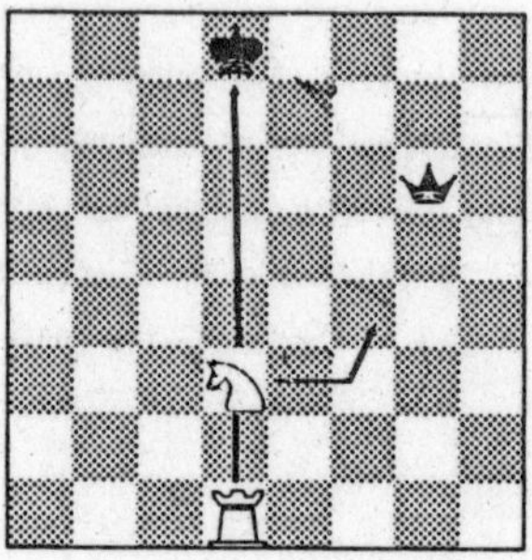

Discovered Check

An attack on the King is uncovered.

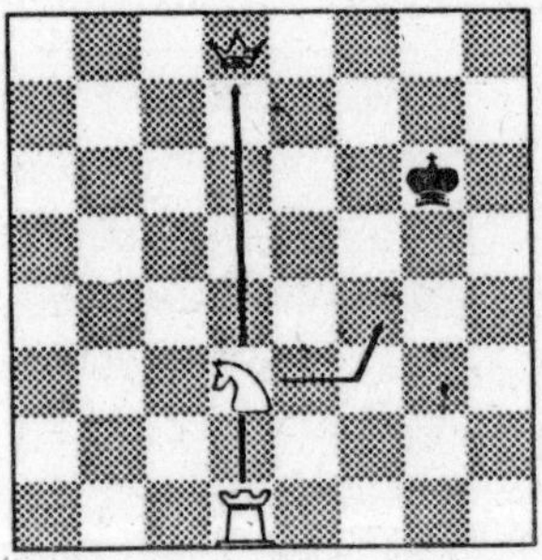

Discovered Attack

One piece, in moving, unmasks the attack of another.

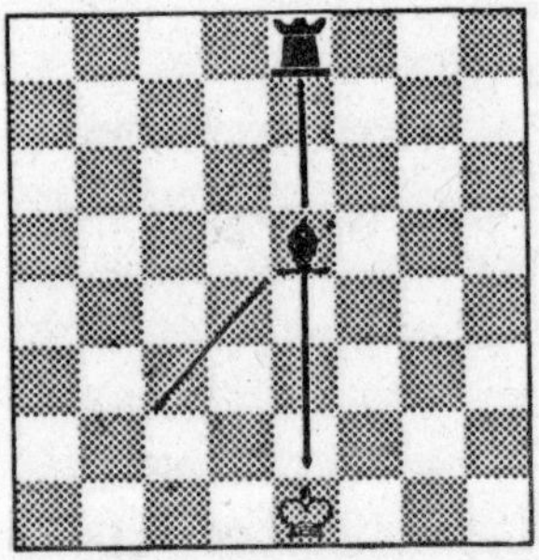

Double Check

One piece unmasks another, both giving checks.

The following four half diagrams show different kinds of double attack.

Queen Fork

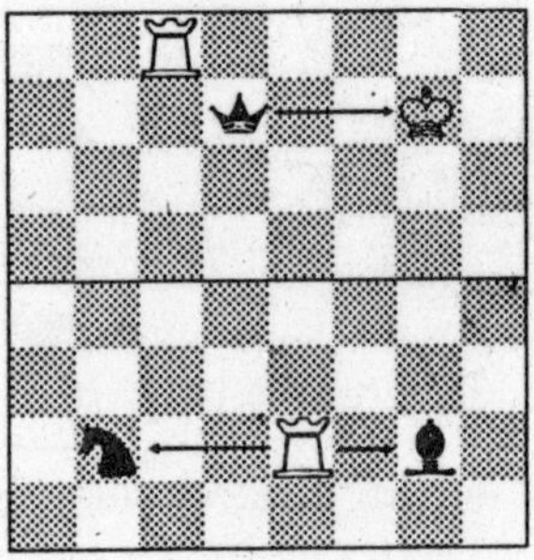

Rook Fork

Bishop Fork

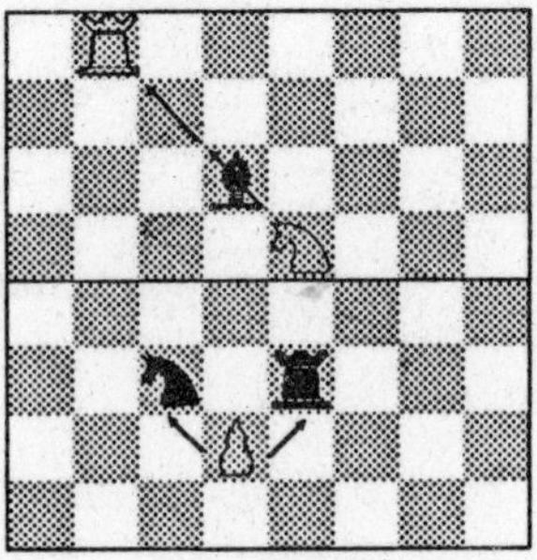

Pawn Fork

The following positions from games show a number of these winning methods in action. Each particular tactical device is explained in greater detail.

1. Tactical Positions

Knight fork: an attack on two or more pieces at the same time.

Black to play

1 ... Qe6×d5+

2 Qd2×d5

Black has given up him Queen for White's Rook—why?

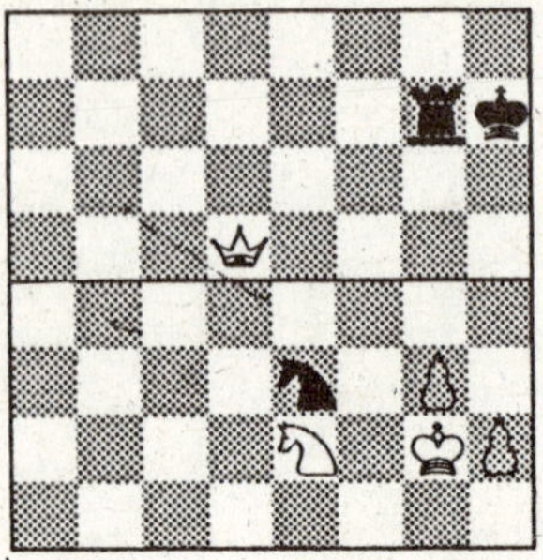

2 ...   Nf5–e3+

Black's Knight forks White's King and Queen. See the diagram above.

3 K any square   Ne3×d5

Black has ended up a whole Rook ahead.

Pin: an attack along a line on a piece which cannot move without exposing another piece to attack.

1 Bd2–c3

This pins Black's Knight against its King.

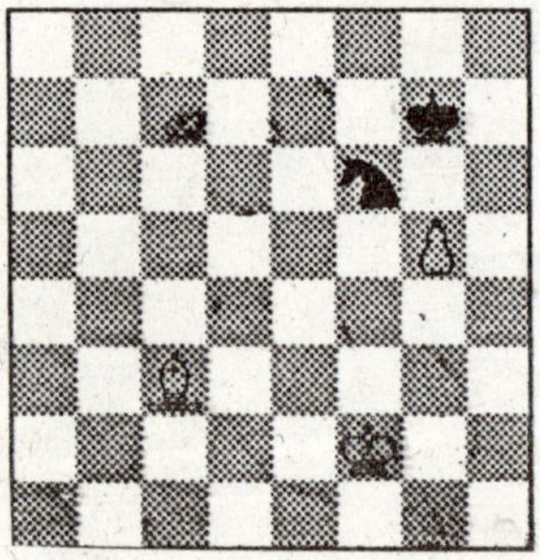

2 g4–g5

Attacking the pinned Knight a second time. See diagram.

1 ... Kh8–g7

Protecting the Knight.

2 ... K any square

3 g5×f6

White wins the Knight.

Skewer: an attack upon two pieces on the same li where the piece nearest the attacker is compelled to mov leaving the other to be taken.

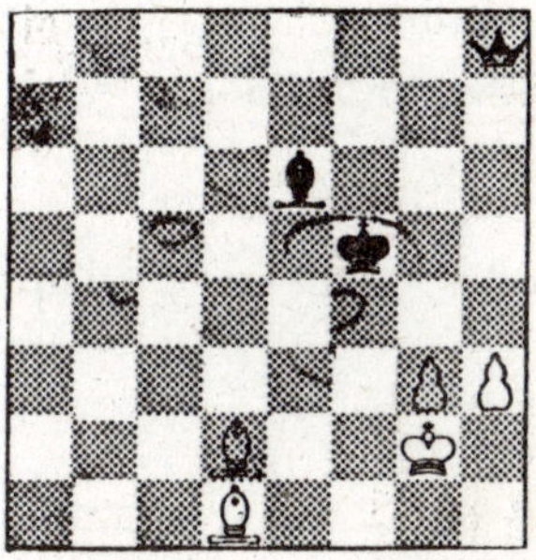

White to play

1 Bd1–c2+ Kf5–e5

The black King has been forced on to the same diagonal as the black Queen. If it had moved to f6 the effect would have been the same.

Now comes the skewer.

2 Bd2–c3+

See diagram.
After the black Kin moves out of check, ther follows:

3 Bc3×h8

Discovered attack: an attack made by uncovering t attacking action of a Queen, Rook or Bishop.

White to play

1 h4–h5+

This is not a check just for the sake of checking. The idea is to drive the black King to either h6 or g7, in either case being exposed to attack by another piece.

1 ... Kg6–g7

2 Nd4–f5+

In checking the black King. White has *uncovered* an attack against the black Queen.

After the King moves out of check, there follows:

3 Rd1×d8

Discovered check: an attack made by uncovering the checking action of a Queen, Rook or Bishop.

White to play

The Bishop on f4 can move, discovering check, but all Black's pieces are on white squares. The Bishop operates on black squares. One enemy piece can be forced on to a black square.

1 a3–a4 Nb5–a7

The Knight moves to the only safe square.

2 Bf4–b8+

Discovering check on the black King by the Rook on f2. 2 Bf4–e3+ would also do equally well.

2 ... K any square

3 Bb8×a7

Double check: a form of discovered check, in which the uncovering piece gives check as well as the piece which is unmasked.

Black to play

In double check the attacked King *must move*—you cannot capture two checking pieces in one move, nor block checks coming from two different directions at once.

1 ... f5–f4+

2 Kg3–h3

The white King has now been forced on to the diagonal commanded by the black Bishop on d7.

2 ... Ng4–f2#

Double checkmate!

The Bishop on d7 and the Knight on f2 work together. Since the white King cannot move from this double check, it is mate.

X

ONE MOVE CHECKMATE END-GAMES: PROBLEMS AND THEIR SOLUTIONS

Given below are more than hundred problems with their solutions. It is advisable for the young learners to solve them first by looking at them and in case they don't find the right move, only then should they look below for the answers.

Normally these problems must have their instant solution in your mind, without your resorting to using the board and the piece. Try to visualise them in your mind and develop this habit for better comprehension of the game.

1

2

3

4

Answers

1. Re8 mate
2. Ra8 mate
3. Rg8 mate
4. Q×g7 mate

5

6

7

8

Answers

5. Nf7 mate
6. Bg7 mate
7. b7 mate
8. R×b8 mate

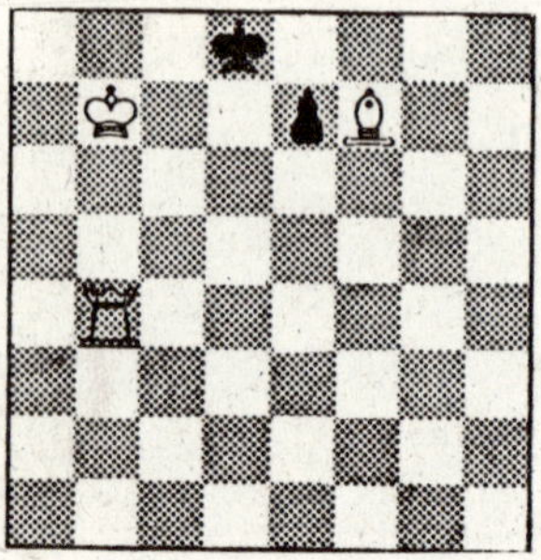

9

10

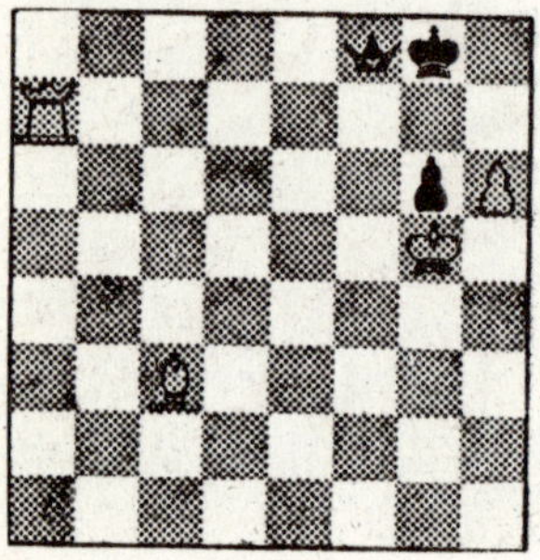

11

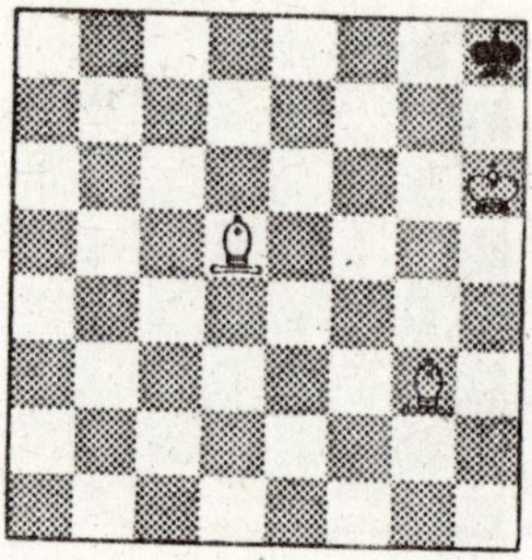

12

Answers

9. Rd4 mate
10. Nh6 mate
11. h7 mate
12. Be5 mate

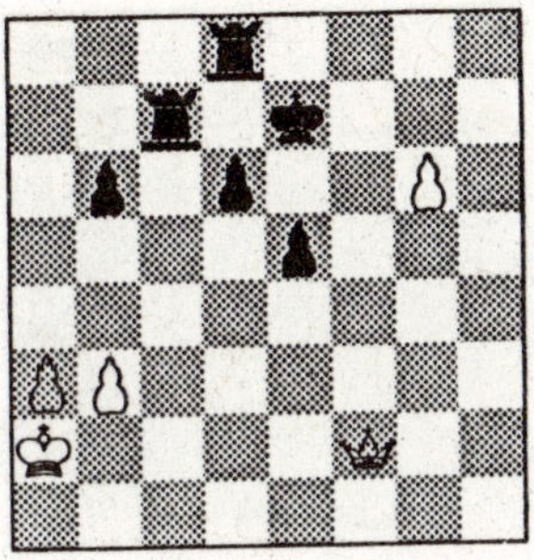

13

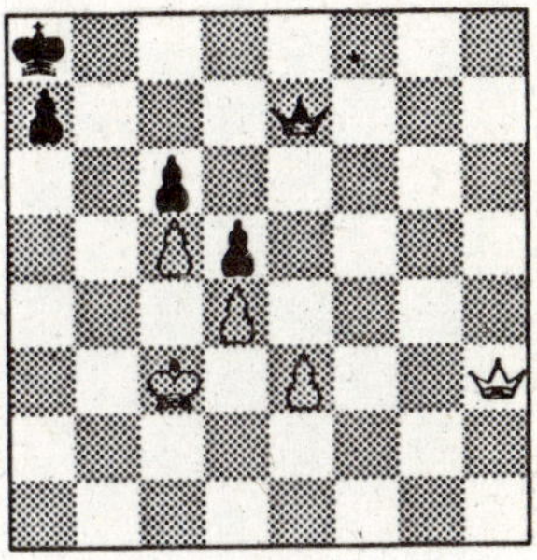

14

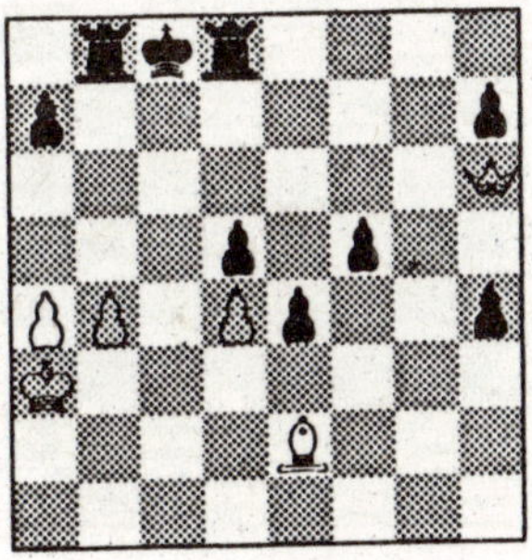

15

16

Answers

13. Qf7 mate
14. Qc8 mate
15. Qc6 mate
16. Qh7 mate

17

18

19

20

Answers

17. Nf7 mate
18. Qf7 mate or Qe8 mate
19. Ra1 mate
20. Rf7 mate

21

22

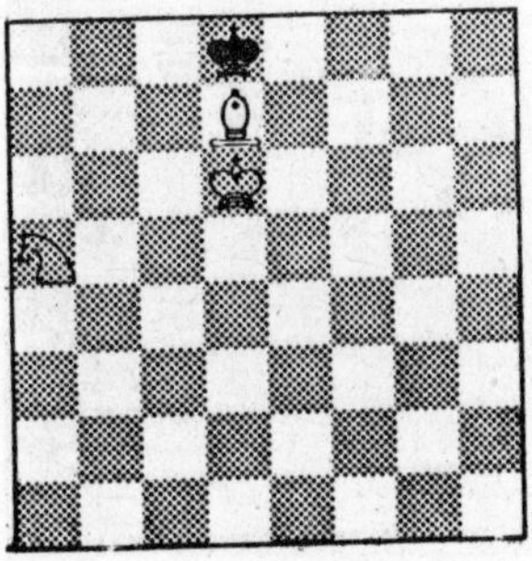

23

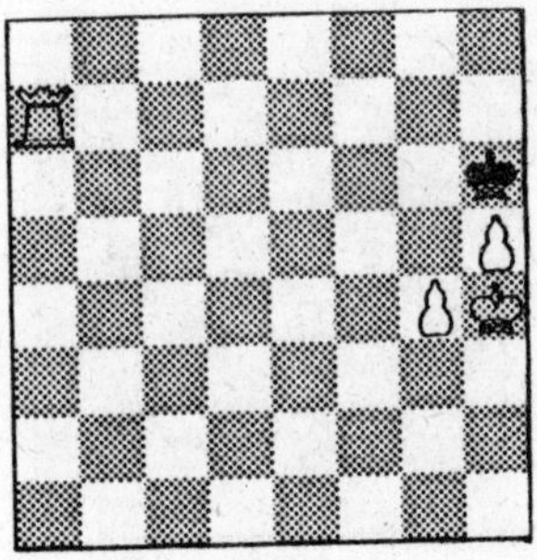

24

Answers

21. Qe7 mate
22. Ra8 mate
23. Nb7 or Nc6 mate
24. g5 mate

25

26

27

28

Answers

25. c8Q mate

26. c8N mate

27. d8Q or d8R mate

28. g8Q or g8R mate

29

30

31

32

Answers

29. d8Q or d8B mate

30. c8N mate (if c×b8Q+ Black plays K×b8)

31. b8Q mate

32. d×e8Q mate

33

34

35

36

Answers

33. Ng6 mate
34. d6 mate
35. Q×h7 mate
36. R×e6 mate

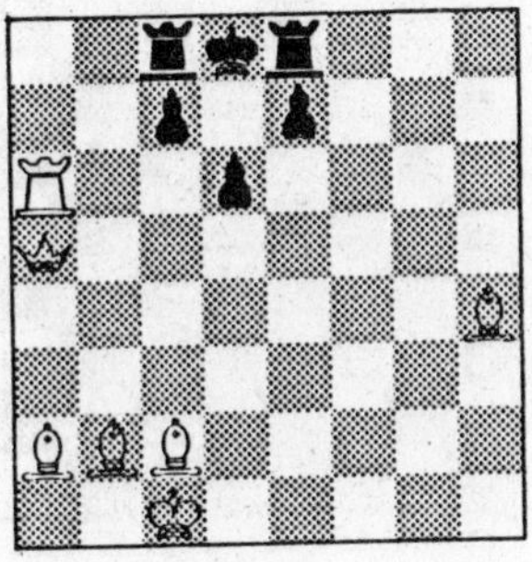

37

38

39

40

Answers

37. Rxd6 mate

38. Nb6 or Nc7 mate

39. Rd8 mate

40. Nxf7 mate

41

42

43

44

Answers

41. Rh5 mate
42. Rd4 mate
43. Qa6 mate
44. Re8 mate

PIN

45

46

47

48

Answers

45. Rxa6 mate

46. Rd8 mate

47. Ng6 mate or Rxf7 mate

48. Ne6 mate

49

50

51

52

Answers

49. Qe5 mate
50. R×h7 mate
51. Re6 mate
52. Bh7 mate

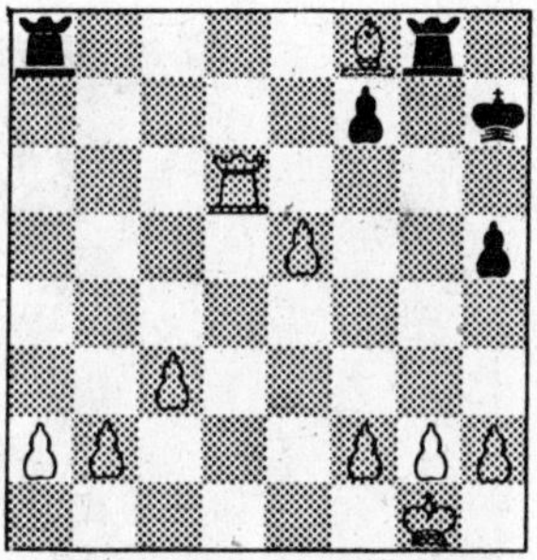

53

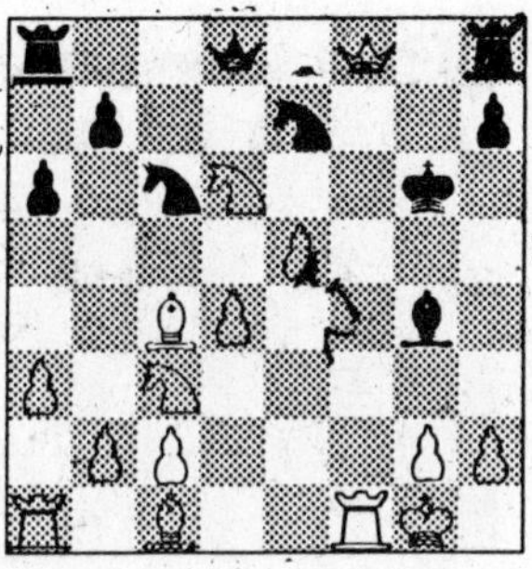

54

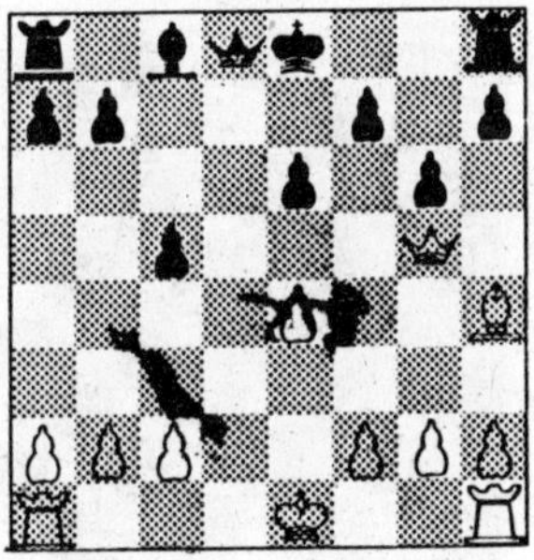

55

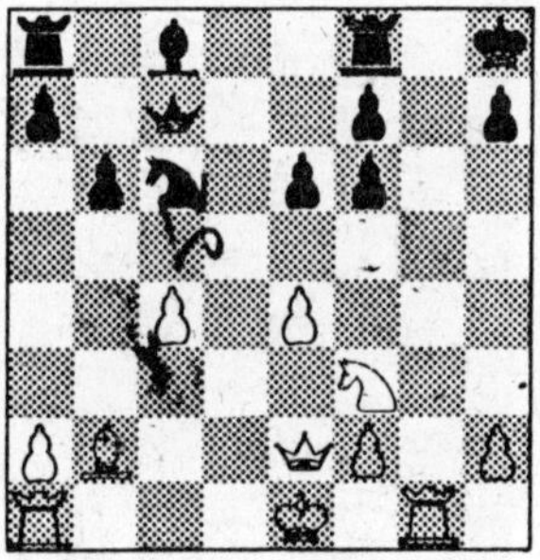

56

Answers

53. Rh6 mate

54. Bf7 mate

55. Q×d8 mate

56. B×f6 mate

57

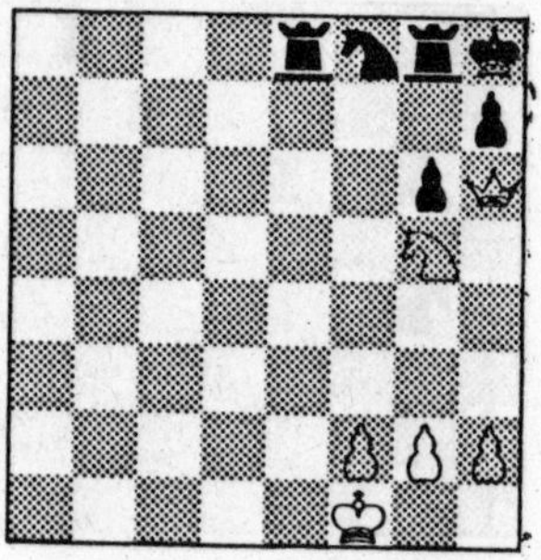

58

59

60

Answers

57. Qh5 mate
58. Nf7 mate
59. Re8 mate
60. Ne7 mate

61

62

63

64

Answers

61. Rh3 mate

62. g3 mate

63. Bh6 mate

64. Ba6 mate

MISCELLANEOUS

65

66

67

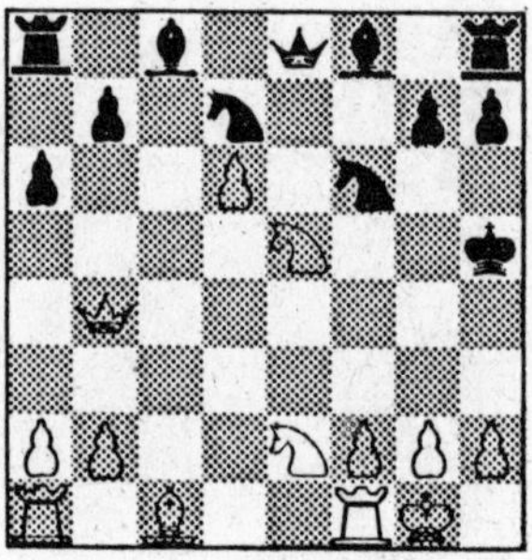

68

Answers

65. Nf4 mate

66. Qf7 mate

67. Qh3 mate

68. Ng3 mate

69

70

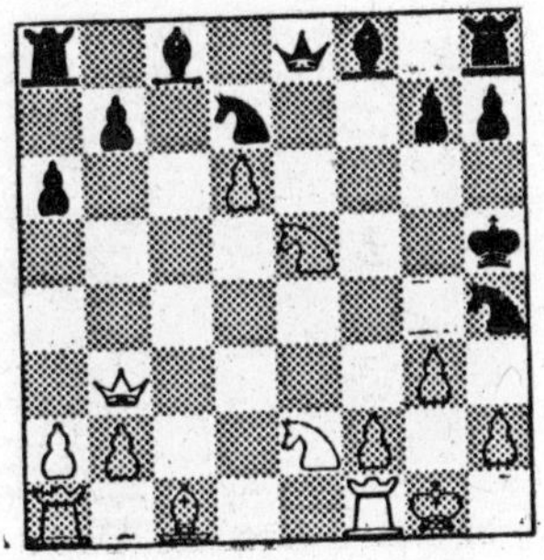

71

72

Answers

69. Qg5 mate

70. Ng3 mate

71. g4 mate

72. Qg4 mate

73

74

75

76

Answers

73. Q×h6 mate

74. Bf6 mate

75. Ra3 mate

76. Qg6 mate

77

78

79

80

Answers

77. Q×h7 mate

78. Ng6 mate

79. Bg6 mate

80. Re8 mate

XI

TWO MOVE CHECKMATE PROBLEMS AND THEIR SOLUTIONS

BACK ROW

1

2

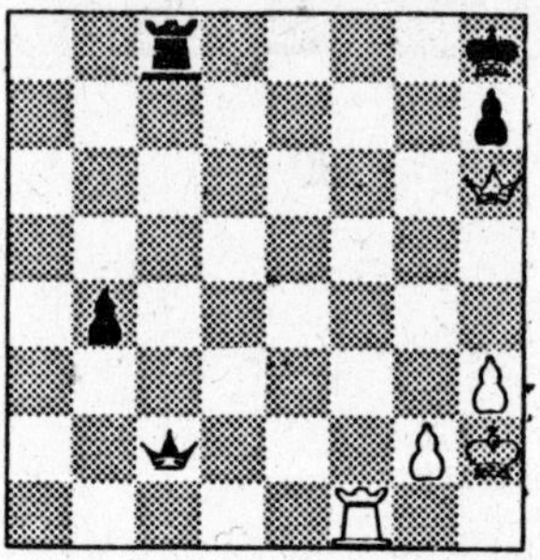

3

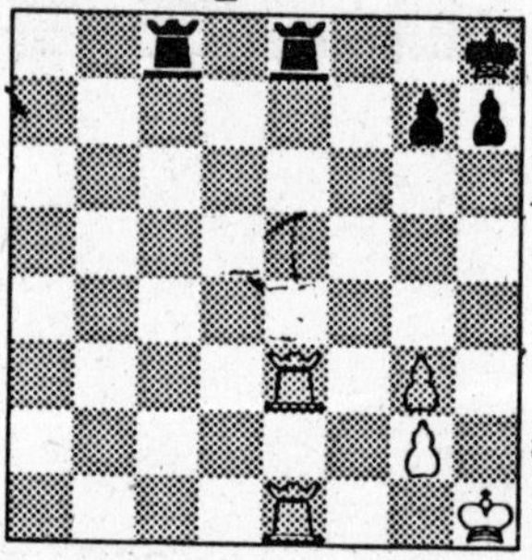

4

Answers

1. 1 Re8+R×e8 2 R×e8 mate
2. 1 Qe8+B×e8 2 R×e8 mate
3. 1 Rf8+R×f8 2 Q×f8 mate
4. 1 R×e8+R×e8 2 R×e8 mate

5

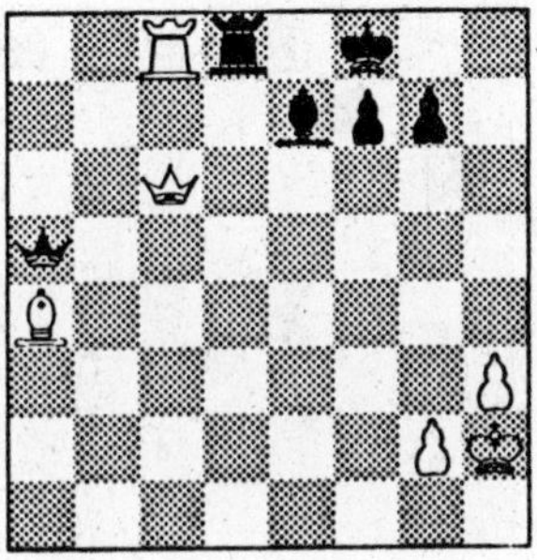

6

7

8

Answers

5. 1 Q×f8+ R×f8 2 R×f8 mate or 1 R×f8+ Rxf8 2 Qxf8 mate

6. 1 Qe8+ R×e8 2 R×e8 mate not 1 R×d8+? Q×d8!

7. 1 Qg8+ R×g8 2 h×g8Q or h×g8R mate (double check!)

8. 1 Q×e8+ R×e8 2 R×e8 mate

9

10

11

12

Answers

9. 1 B×d4+ R×d4 2 Rf8 mate

10. 1 Re8+ Bf8 2 either R×f8 mate

11. 1 Ra8+ B×a8 2 Qc8 mate

12. 1 Rd8+ Bf8 2 R×f8 mate

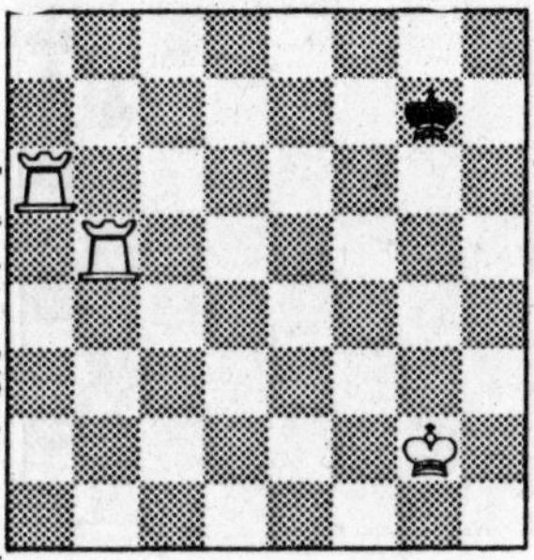

13

14

15

16

Answers

13. 1 Rb7+ followed by Ra8 mate

14. 1 R×e8+ R×e8 2 R×e8 mate

15. 1 Rg3+ followed by Rc8 mate

16. 1 Be4+ followed by Rd8 mate

17

18

19

20

Answers

17. 1 Ng6+ h×g6 2 Rh1 mate
18. 1 R×h7+ K×h7 2 Rh1 mate
19. 1 Be6+ Kh8 2 R×f8 mate
20. 1 Qd8+! K×d8 2 Rf8 mate

21

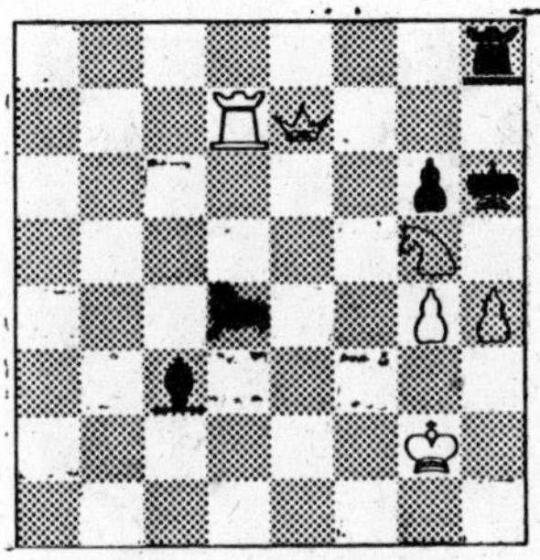

22

23

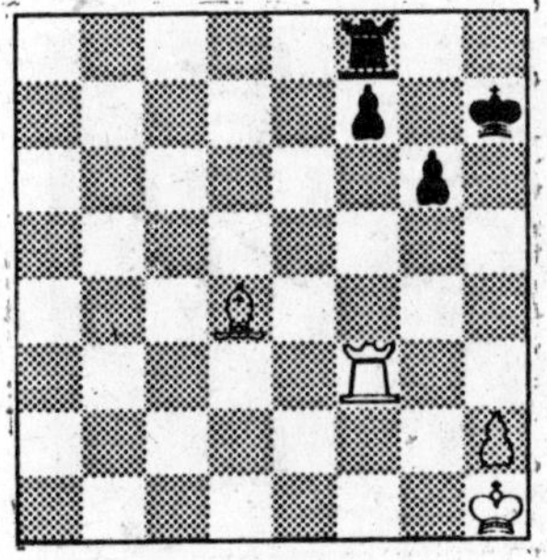

24

Answers

21. 1 Nf6+ Kh8 2 R×g8 mate

22. 1 Qh7+ R×h7 2 R×h7 mate

23. 1 Q×h7+ K×h7 2 Rh3 mate

24. 1 Rh3+ Kg8 2 Rh8 mate

25

26

27

28

Answers

25. 1 Qf8+ R×f8 2 R×f8 mate

26. 1 Q×h7+ K×h7 2 Rh5 mate

27. 1 Q×e8+ K×e8 2 Rd8 mate

28. 1 Qc8+ B×c8 2 R×c8 mate or 1 Qc8+ Be8 2 Q×e8 mate

BACK ROW

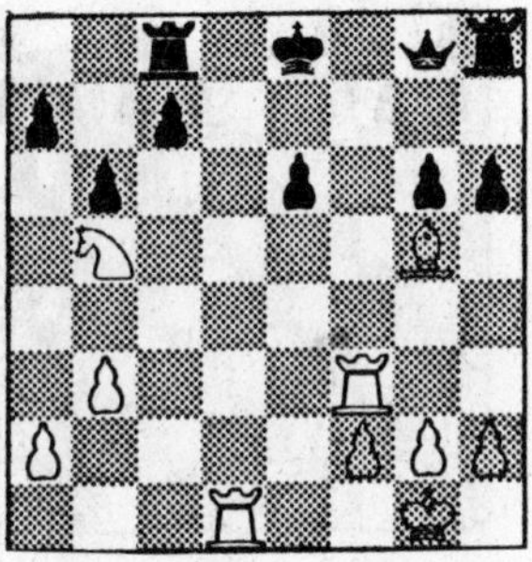

29

30

31

32

Answers

29. 1 N×c7+ R×c7 2 Rd8 mate

30. 1 B×h7+ Kh8 2 R×f8 mate

31. 1 Rh4+ Kg8 2 Rh8 mate

32. 1 Re8+ N×e8 2 Rf8 mate

33

34

35

36

Answers

33. 1 R×f8+ K×f8 2 Re8 mate

34. 1 Qd8+ B×d8 2 Re8 mate

35. 1 Q×h7+ K×h7 2 Rh3 mate

36. 1 Nc5+ Ke8 2 Rf8 mate

BACK ROW

37

38

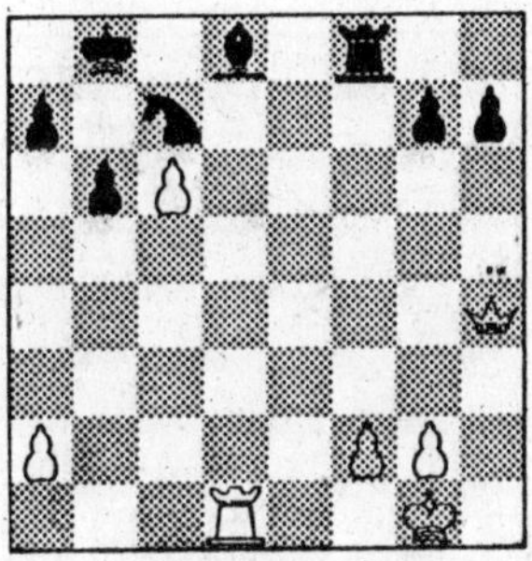

39

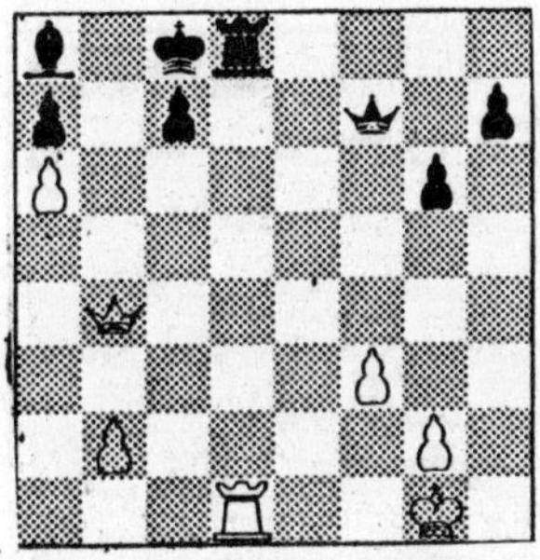

40

Answers

37. 1 Qf8+ R×f8 2 R×f8 mate

38. 1 R×f8+ Q×f8 2 Q×f8 mate

39. 1 R×d8+ R×d8 2 Q×d8 mate or
1 Q×d8+ R×d8 2 R×d8 mate

40. 1 Qb8+ K×b8 2 R×d8 mate

41

42

43

44

Answers

41. 1 Rg8+ R×g8 2 R×g8 mate

42. 1 Q×h7+ K×h7 2 Rh3 mate

43. 1 Rg7+ Kg8 2 Rh8 mate

44. 1 F×g7+ Kg8 2 Rf8 mate

BACK ROW

45

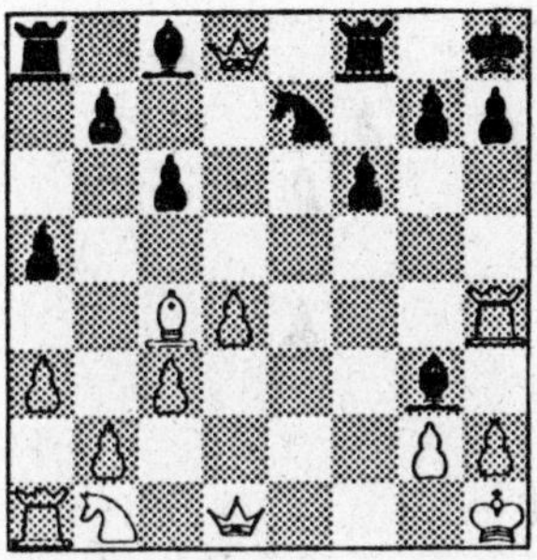

46

47

48

Answers

45. 1 Q×f7+ R×f7 2 Re8 mate or
1 Q×f7+ Kh8 2 Q×f8 mate

46. 1 R×h7+ K×h7 2 Qh5 mate

47. 1 Q×h7+ K×h7 2 Rh4 mate

48. 1 Q×h7+ R×h7 2 Rg8 mate

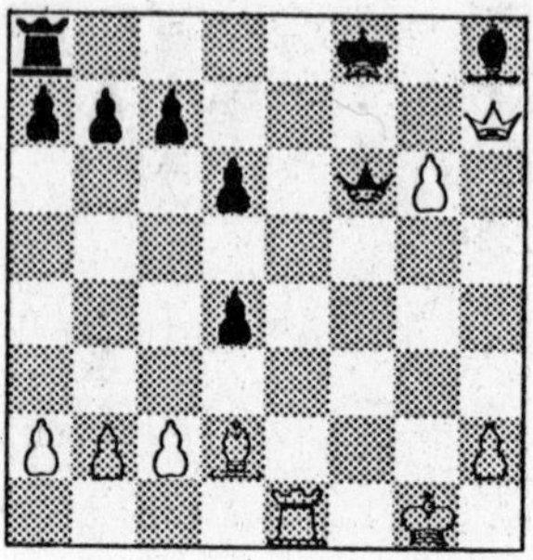

49

50

51

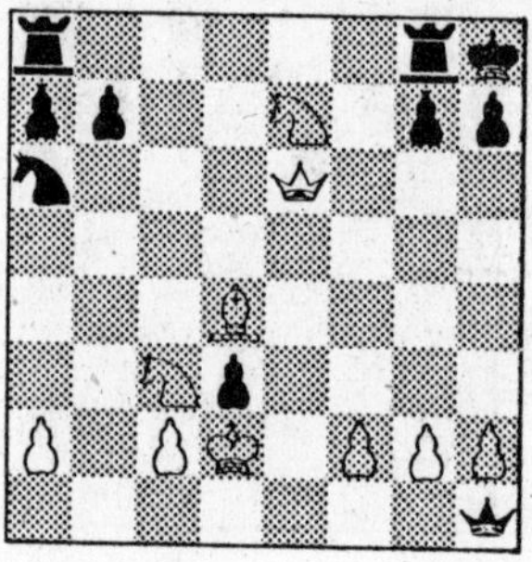

52

Answers

49. 1 Bh6+ Bg7 2 Qh8 mate or
1 Bh6+ Qg7 2 Q×h8 mate

50. 1 R×h6+ K×h6 2 Qh8 mate

51. 1 R×g8+ R×g8 2 Nh7 mate or
1 Nh7+ R×h7 2 R×g8 mate

52. 1 Ng6+ H×g6 2 Qh3 mate

53

54

55

56

Answers

53. 1 Rh5+ G×h5 2 Q×h5 mate

54. 1 Qa8+ R×a8 2 R×a8 mate

55. 1 R×f8+ K×f8 2 Qd8 mate

56. 1 Qg5+ Kf8 2 Qg8 mate or 1 Q×h7+! Kf8 2 Qg8 mate or 1 Q×h7+ K×f6 2 Qh6 mate!

57

58

59

60

Answers

57. 1 Bd5+ Kh8 or Kh7 2 Rh2 mate

58. 1 Rh8+ B×h8 2 Q×h8 mate

59. 1 Q×h7+ K×h7 2 Rh4 mate

60. 1 Q×h6+ K×h6 2 Rh8 mate or
1 Rh8+ K×h8 2 Q×h6 mate

BACK ROW

61

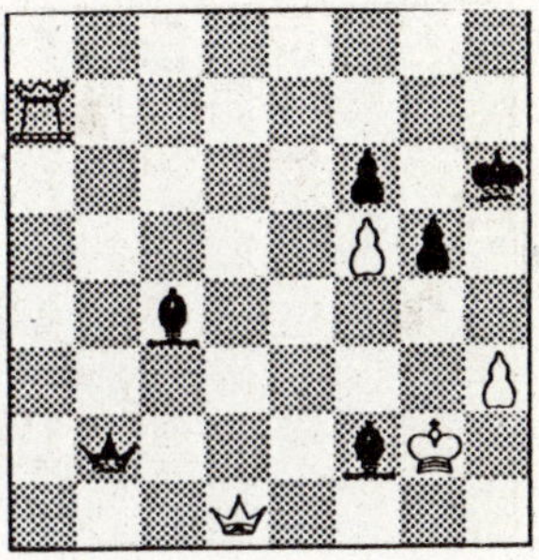

62

63

64

Answers

61. 1 Ng6+ H×g6 2 Rh1 mate

62. 1 Qh5+ K×h5 2 Rh7 mate

63. 1 Qe8+ Rg8 2 Q×g8 or R×g8 mate

64. 1 Qf8+ Kh7 2 Qg7 mate or 1 Qf8+ B×f8 2 Rh8 mate

65

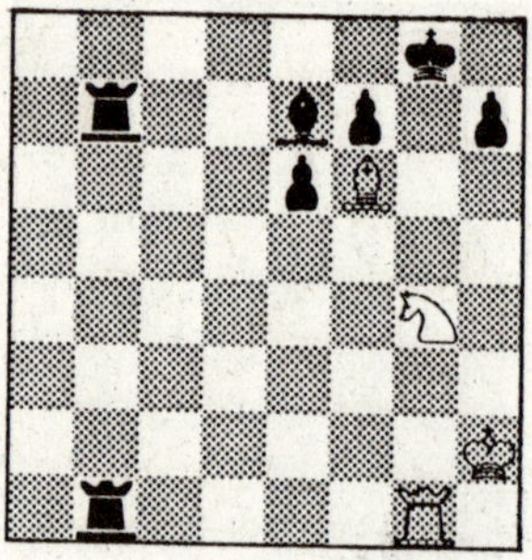

66

67

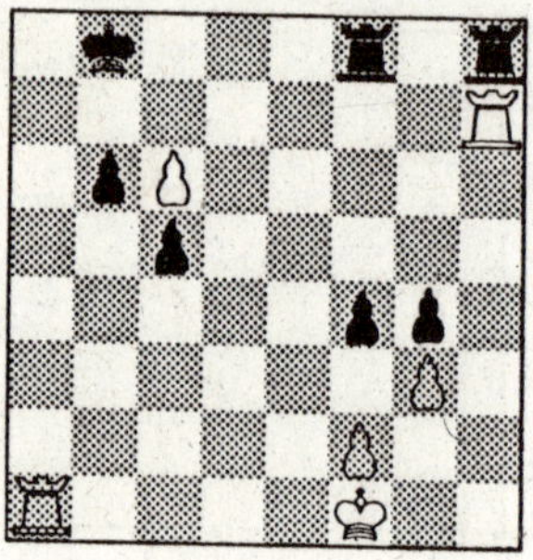

68

Answers

65. 1 Ng5+ Kg8 or Kh8 2 Rd8 mate

66. 1 Nh6+ Kf8 2 Rg8 mate

67. 1 Rc8+ Rb7 2 Rf7 mate

68. 1 Rb7+ Kc8 2 Ra8 mate

BACK ROW

69

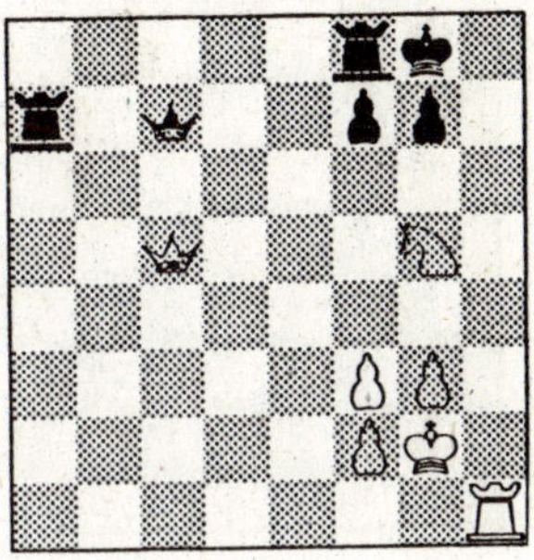

70

71

72

Answers

69. 1 Be6+ Kh8 2 R×f8 mate

70. 1 Rh8+ K×h8 2 Q×f8 mate

71. 1 Q×f7+ Kh8 2 Q×f8 mate or
1 Q×f7+ R×f7 2 Rd8 mate

72. 1 R×h7+ R×h7 2 Qf8 mate

73

74

75

76

Answers

73. 1 Q×f8+ K×f8 2 Ra8 or Rb8 mate

74. 1 Qe8+ Bf8 2 Q×f8 mate

75. 1 Bc5+ followed by Re8 mate

76. 1 Bh6+ Kg8 2 R×e8 mate

77

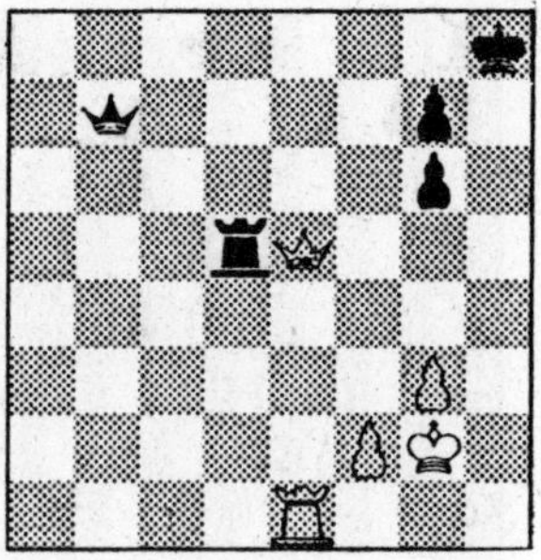

78

79

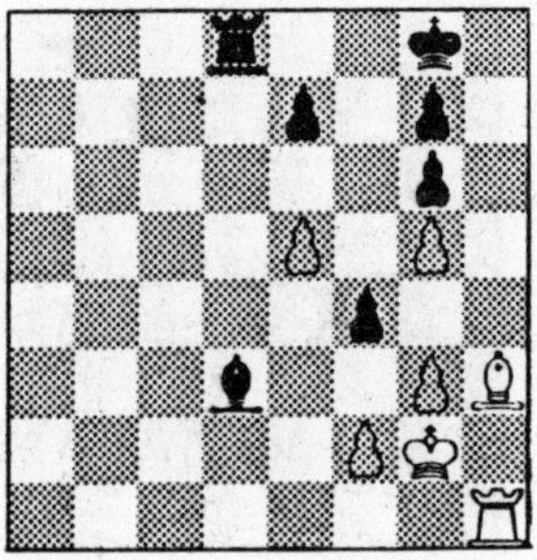

80

Answers

77. 1 Qg8+ K×g8 2 Re8 mate

78. 1 Qe8+? Kh7 2 Rh1+ Rh5+!! but
1 Rh1+! Kg8 2 Qe8 mate!

79. 1 Ng6+ Kg8 2 R×f8 mate

80. 1 Be6+ Kf8 2 Rh8 mate

81

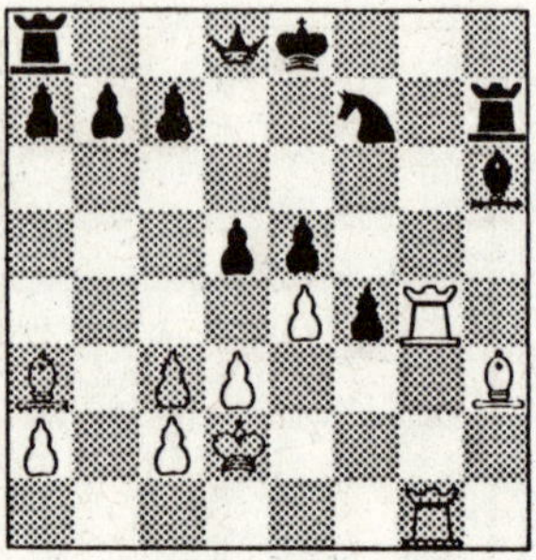

82

83

84

Answers

81. 1 Rg8+ R×g8 2 R×g8 mate

82. 1 Rg8+ Bf8 2 R×f8 mate

83. 1 Re8+ B×e8 2 R×e8 mate

84. 1 Qa8+ Qc8 2 Q×c8 mate

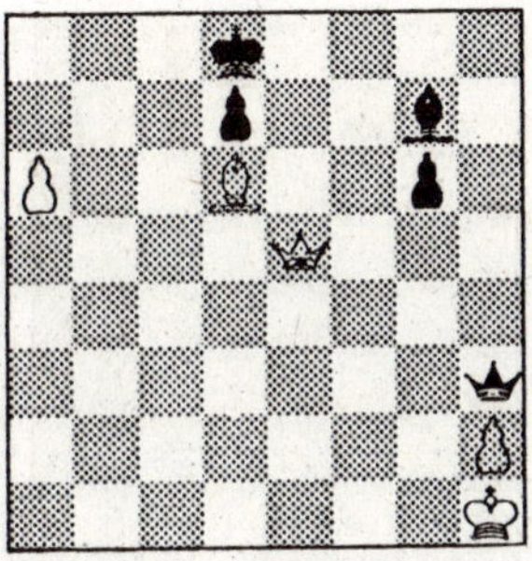

85

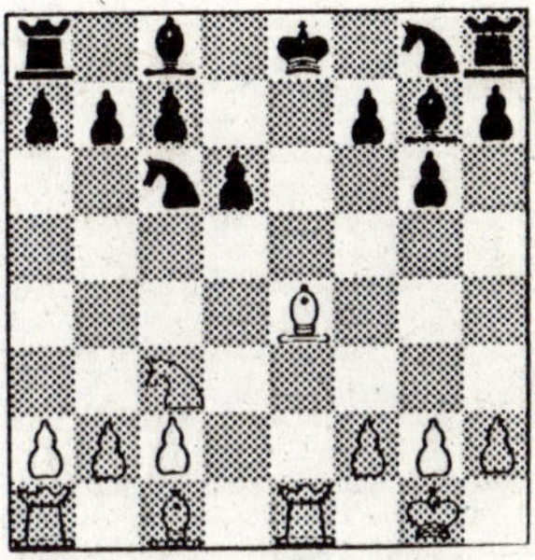

86

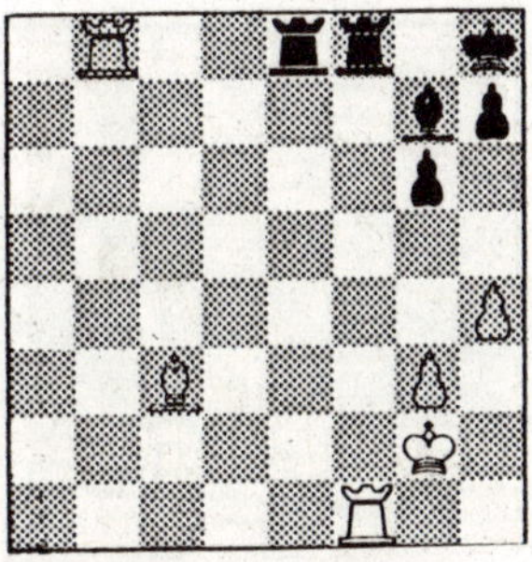

87

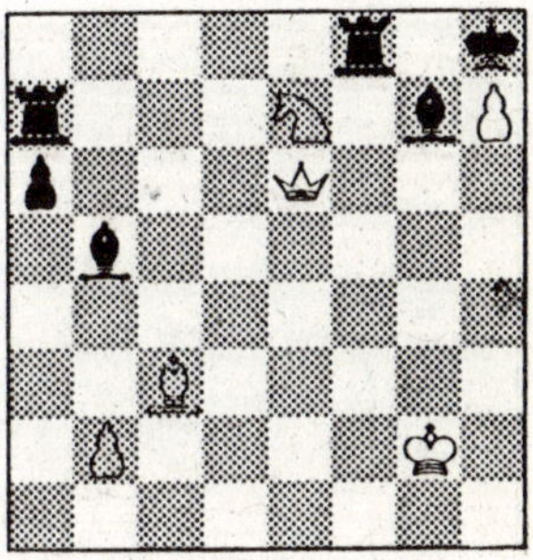

88

Answers

85. 1 Qe7+ Kc8 2 Qe8 mate

86. 1 B×c6+ followed by Re8 mate

87. 1 R×f8+ R×f8 2 R×f8 mate

88. 1 Qg8+ R×g8 2 h×g8Q mate

89

90

91

92

Answers

89. 1 Rh8+ B×h8 2 R×h8 mate
90. 1 Qh8+ R×h8 2 R×h8 mate
91. 1 H×g6+ (double check!) Kg8 2 Rh8 mate
92. 1 Qc4+ Kh8 2 Qc8 mate

QUEEN

93

94

95

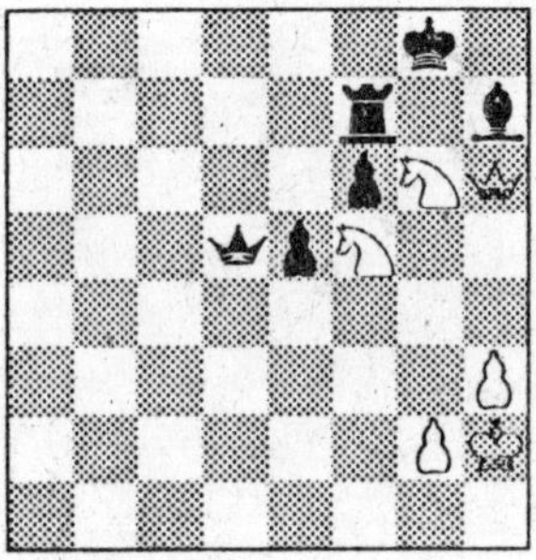

96

Answers

93: 1 Qh7+ Kf8 2 Q×f7 mate

94: 1 Ne7+ Kh8 2 Q×f8 mate

95: 1 Qd3+ Ke6 2 Qd7 mate

96: 1 Nfe7+ R×e7 2 Qf8 mate or
1 Qg7+ R×g7 2 Nh6 mate

97

98

99

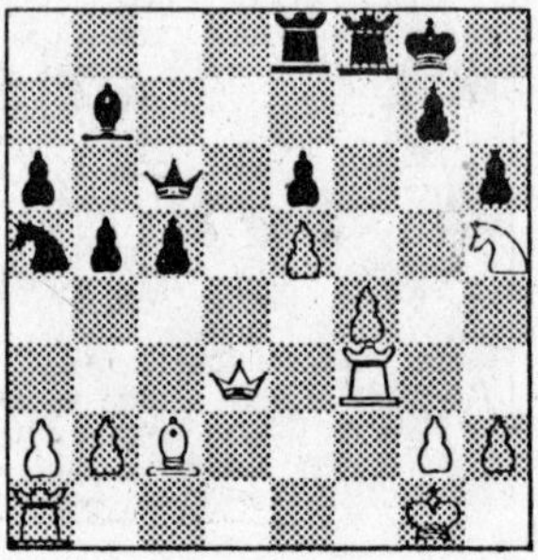

100

Answers

97. 1 Ne6+ Ke8 2 Qd8 mate

98. 1 B×e6+ followed by Q×h7 mate or
1 B×h7+ Kh8 2 Nf7 mate

99. 1 Q×g6+ followed by either Q×g7 or Qh7 mate

100. 1 Qh7+ Kf7 2 Q×g7 mate

101

102

103

104

Answers

101. 1 Rg8+ K×g8 2 Qg7 or Qh8 mate

102. 1 Q×h5+ Nh6 2 Q×h6 mate

103. 1 Rf7+ Kg8 2 Qe8 mate

104. 1 R×g8+ K×g8 2 Qe8 mate

105

106

107

108

Answers

105. 1 Nf7+ Kd7 2 Bb5 mate

106. 1 Rd8+ Rg8 2 c4 mate

107. 1 Bf6+ Kf8 2 Nh7 mate or 1 Bf6+ Kg6 2 Bf7 mate

108. 1 Q×e6+ f×e6 2 Bg6 mate

109

110

111

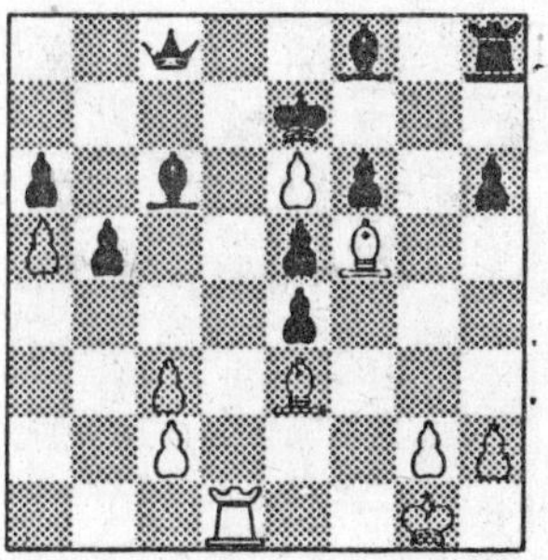

112

Answers

109. 1 Bf5+ Kc7 2 Bd8 mate

110. 1 h6+ K×h6 2 Bf8 mate

111. 1 Rf8+ Kg7 2 Bh6 mate

112. 1 Bc5+ Ke8 2 Bg6 mate

113

114

115

116

Answers

113. 1 Ne4+ Kh4 2 Bf6 or Bg3 mate

114. 1 Kf8 followed by Bc3 mate

115. 1 g4+ Kh4 2 Be1 mate

116. 1 Q×f7+ R×f7 2 B×f7 mate or
1 B×f7+ R×f7 2 Q×f7 mate

117

118

119

120

Answers

117. 1 Bf4+ Kd7 2 Be6 mate

118. 1 Q×g4+ K×g4 2 Be2 mate

119. 1 Q×c6+ b×c6 2 Ba6 mate

120. 1 Bd5+ Ne6 2 B×e6 mate or

1 Bd5+ B×d5 2 Rf8 mate

KNIGHT

121

122

123

124

Answers

121. 1 Rf8+ R×f8 2 Ng7 mate

122. 1 Rd×d8+ Q×d8 2 Ne7 mate

123. 1 Qg8+ R×g8 2 Nf7 mate

124. 1 R×h6+ Kg8 2 Ne7 mate

KNIGHT

125

126

127

128

Answers

125. 1 Nfh6+ N×h6 2 N×h6 mate but not
1 Ngh6+? Kh7 2 Ne7+ B×c2

126. 1 Qe7+ Kg8 2 Nh6 mate

127. 1 Nh6+ Kf8 2 Nh7 mate

128. 1 Qh8+ B×h8 2 Nh7 mate or
1 Ne6+ F×e6 2 Q×g7 mate

129

130

131

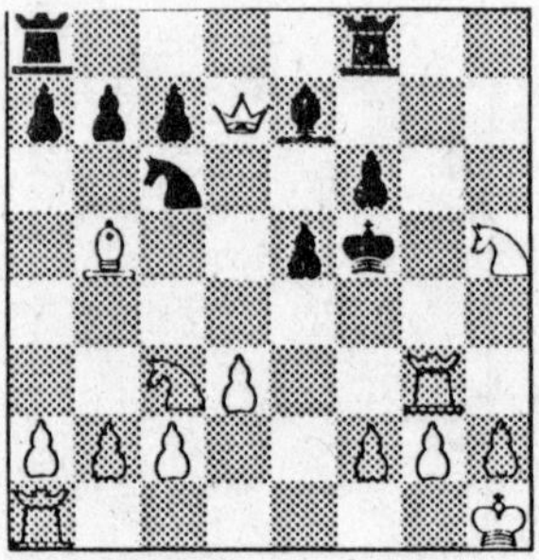

132

Answers

129. 1 R×f7+ N×f7 2 Ng6 mate

130. 1 Q×h7+ Q×h7 2 Nf7 mate

131. 1 either Ne6+ N×e6 2 N×e6 mate

132. 1 Ng7+ Kf4 2 Ne2 mate

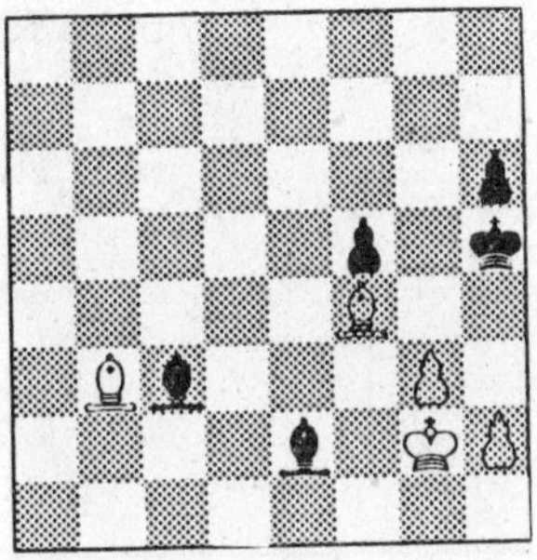

133

134

135

136

Answers

133. 1 Bf7+ Kg4 2 h3 mate

134. 1 R×h7+ Kg5 2 h4 mate

135. 1 Nh4+ Ke6 2 d5 mate

136. 1 d5+ c×d5 2 c×d5 mate

137

138

139

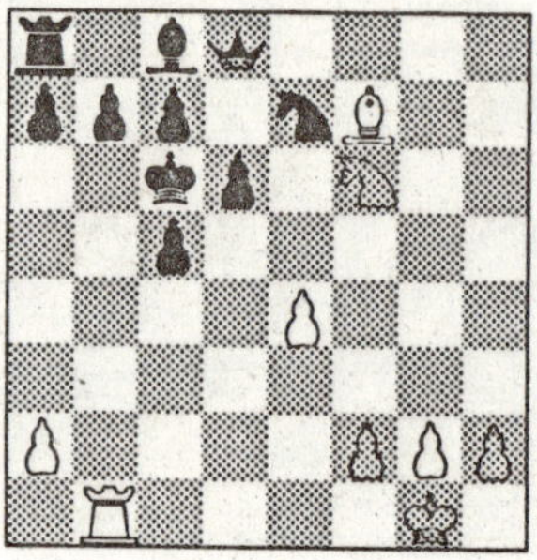

140

Answers

137. 1 Bf7+ N×f7 2 e×f7 mate

138. 1 Qf7+ R×f7 2 e×f7 mate

139. 1 Qg6+! N×g6 2 f×g6 mate

140. 1 Bd5+ N×d5 2 e×d5 mate

141

142

143

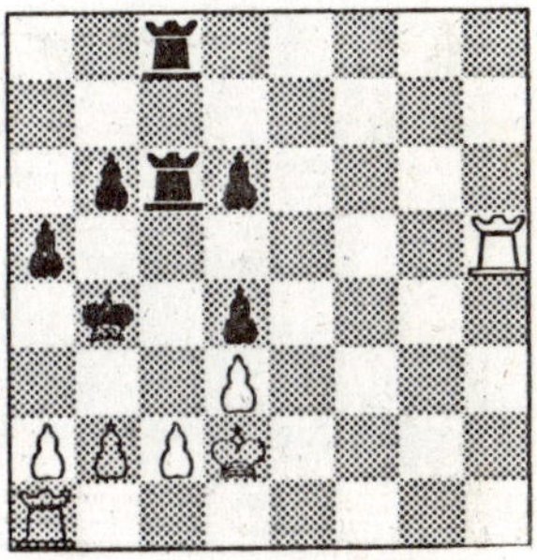

144

Answers

141. 1 Rh8! b6 2 a×b6 mate or

1 Rh8! b5 2 a×b6 en passant, mate

142. 1 Q×c3+ N×c3 2 b4 mate

143. 1 Bc7+ Ka7 2 b6 mate

144. 1 a3+ Ka4 2 b3 mate

145

146

147

148

Answers

145. 1 Rh8+ K×h8 2 Qh7 mate or
1 Rh8+ Q×h8 2 Qf7 mate

146. 1 B×a6 and mate next move by either Qc7 or Qd8 depending upon Black's move

147. 1 R×g7+ K×g7 or Kh8 2 Q×h7 mate

148. 1 Rg7+ K×g7 2 Qh7 mate

149

150

151

152

Answers

149. 1 N×h7+ N×h7 2 Ng6 mate

150. 1 N×a7+ Kd7 2 Bb5 mate

151. 1 Qf8+ R×f8 2 R×f8 mate

152. 1 Rb8+ N×b8 2 Qb7 mate or
1 R×c7+ and Qb7 mate

153

154

155

156

Answers

153. 1 R×h6+ g×h6 2 Qf7 mate!

154. 1 R×f7+ K×f7 2 Qg7 mate

155. 1 R×b6+ Ka7 2 Qb7 mate or
1 R×c7+ Kb8 2 Qb7 mate

156. 1 Qh7+ Kf8 2 Qg8 mate or
1 Qh7+ K×f6 2 Q×h6 mate

157

158

159

160

Answers

157. 1 Ng6+ h×g6 2 Qh3 mate

158. 1 Nd6+ either N×d6 2 Q×b8 mate or
1 Nd6+ Q×d6 2 Qb7 mate

159. 1 Rh8+ K×h8 2 Qh7 mate

160. 1 Qf8+ Bg8 2 Q×f6 mate

XII

SOME QUIZ PROBLEMS

Given below are some problems especially created to test your ability in chess as by now you must be knowing at the Masters' category gates! These problems are by no means difficult but some what tricky. By solving these in one go you deem yourself to be able to defeat your club champion. Their solutions are given in the end. But before rushing to see them you must try to solve independently.

Problem No. 1

White to move and win

Problem No. 2

White to move and draw

Problem No. 3

White to move and win

Problem No. 4

White to move and win in Seven Moves

Problem No. 5

White to move and win in Three Moves

Problem No. 6

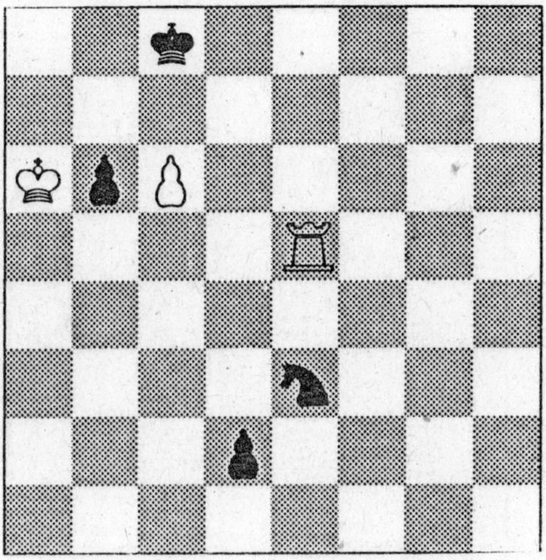

White to move and draw

Problem No. 7

White to move and draw

Problem No. 8

White to move and win

INDEX TO THE ABBREVIATIONS AND SIGNS USED IN THE SOLUTIONS

+	Check, Checks, Checker	K	King
dis+	Discovered Check	Sq.	Square
++	Double Check	Di	Diagonal
P	Pawn	×	Take, Takes, Took
R	Rook	Inc	Mating Combination
N	Knight		
B	Bishop	pc	Piece
Q	Queen	e.p.	"en passant" (in passing)

SOLUTION TO THE QUIZ PROBLEMS

Solution to Problem No. 1

I. 1. h7+–K×h7

2. Ba4–R×b2+

3. Be2+–R×c2+

4. Kf3–Rc3+

5. Kf4–Rc4+

6. Kf5–(a)

(a) Black can + any more and White's e7 queens and White wins

This is the author's solution. This sacrifices both Bs and a P and makes winning a prolonged affairs with White's Q against two Ps and R of Black.

However, White can win with logical moves in 7, or 5, or 3 or even 2 as under:

II. 1. Bg6(b)–R×b2+

2. Kf3–Rb3+

3. Ke4–Rb4+

4. Kd5–Rb5(c)

5. h7+–Kg7(d)

6. e8 = Q–Rb

7. h8 = Q+–Mate

(b) Saves B and protects P when h7+

(c) Protects c5, if Rd4+, K×c5

(d) Threatens K×B. If Kh8, e8 = Q+

III. 1. Bg6–R×b2+

2. Kf3–Rb6(e)

3. h7+–Kh8

4. e8 = Q+–Kg7

5. h8 = Q+–Mate (f)

(e) R attacks other B.

(f) this is win in five moves.

IV. 1. Bg6–R×b2+

2. Kf3–Rb7(g)

3. e8 = Q+–Mate!

(g) A mistake. Black should know that he will not get move to take e7 and that e8 now is Mate!

This is win in 3 moves

V. 1. Bg6–c4(h)

2. h7+–Mate!

(h) Here Black prevents queening of e7. But that was not necessary to mate as White's B at b2 was not taken! This is win in 2 moves

VI. In II above, if, in the 4th move, Black plays—

4. ......Rb8, controlling the 8th rank to prevent queening of e7;

5. K×c5–a5

6. Kc6–Rc8+

7. Kd7–Ra8

8. Kc7–a4

9. Kb7–

Now the R of Black cannot move to any sq. on the 8th rank and will have to come down. Otherwise it will be taken by K. The moment that R comes down.

10. e8 = Q+–Kg7

11. h8 = Q+–Mate!

Solution to Problem No. 2

1. a7–Ra6	2. Kb7–R×a7+
3. K×a7–Nb5+	4. N×b5–g3
5. Rf1+–Kg2	6. Rb1–Kh3
7. Na3–g2	8. Rb+–

After White's 8th move, Black has to move the K and wherever K moves, White gives perpetual +, keeping R on b– file only.

Hence DRAW.

Solution to Problem No. 3

It is an excellent composition, requiring forethought in selecting the moves.

1. Qh4+ White can + by Qe3, Qh2 or Qb4, but he has selected this as Black K can make only one move —Ke5. The K cannot take f3, as then White's Qh5+gets Black's Q1.

1. ...... Ke5 (only)

2. d4+ A beautiful move! If now, 2 .... –K×d4, 3. Qd8+ gets Black's Q. If 2 ... –Q×d4, 3. Qh8+–f6 4. Qh2+– Mate!

2. .... – Kd6 (only)

3. Qd8+–Kc6 (only)

4. a4-Threat is next Qc7+ is mate!-if a4 is not taken 4... –Q×a4

5. Qe8+– Black's K moves and White takes Black's Q and wins the game with his Q easily.

Solution to Problem No. 4

1.	Qd8+–Kh6(a)	(a) To enable Black's Q×g7+ mate?
2.	Qe7(b)–Qb8+	(b) Prevents Q×g7+
3.	g8 = Q–Qb2+	
4.	Qg7+–Q×g7+	
5.	Q×g7+–Kh5 (only)	
6.	Kg8–Kh4 (only)	
7.	h8 = R+– Mate	

Solution to Problem No. 5

I.	1.	Qe5(a)–g4(b)	(a) The Q is saved from the attacking P.
	2.	N×R–B×e4	
	3.	Q×e4+–Mate!	(b) To take Q by R.
II.	1.	Qe5–d6(c)	(c) Attacks Q
	2.	Q×e6!!–R×e6	
	3.	Nd5+– Mate	
III.	1.	Qe5–g×14	
	2.	Q×f4+– Mate!	
IV.	1.	Qe5–R×c8	
	2.	d5–ed	
	3.	N×d5 or Qd4+– Mate	
V.	1.	Qe5–R×c8	
	2.	d5–g×f4	

3. Qd4 +– Mate

VI. 1. Qe5–R×c8

2. d5–B×e4

3. Q×e4 +– Mate

VII 1. Qe5–R×c8

2. d5–R×c5

3. Qd4 +– Mate

White will have to change his moves according to the moves of the Black.

Solution to Problem No. 6

I. 1. Kh5–Kd8

2. K×h6–Nd6+

3. Kb7–Nd6+

4. Kb8–d1 = Q

5. c7+–Kd7

6. c8 = Q+–N×c8

7. Rd5+–Q×d5

(a) If Black plays - d1 = Q here, White will win as shown in III below. Hence Black will not stalemate, as White cannot move his K and no + given.

II. 1. Kb5–e1 = Q

2. Re8+–Kc7 (only)

3. Re7+–Kd8

4. Rd7+–Ke8

5. R×d1–N×d1

6. K×b5–Nc3

7. c7–Nd6+

8. Kb7–N×c7

9. K×c7–DRAW!

However, if

III. 1. Kb5–Kd8

2. K×b6–d1 = Q

3. C7+–Kc8

4. Re8+–Kd7

5. Rd8+–Ke7

6. R×d1–N×d1

7. c8 = Q and White wins!

Solution to Problem No. 7

1. Bf6–gf(a)

2. Be5+–Kc6

3. Bh2–Be6(b)

4. Ke7–Kd5

5. Nf6+–Kd4

6. g6–fg

7. K×eb–Ke3

8. Nd5+–Kf3

9. Nf4(c)–g5

(a) If Black plays h2. White will move Be5+ and take the P.

(b) Takes care of all his Ps.

(c) Attacks g6 and h3!

10. N×h3–Kg2(d) (d) To get one pc.

11. N×g5–K×h2

12. K×f5–DRAW, as neither ride can win.

Solution to Problem No. 8

1. Nd5(a)–Qd8(b)

2. g3(c)–Qa5

3. e6(d)–Qa2+

4. Ke3–Qa5(e)

5. Kf4–Qd2+ (f)

6. Kf5 –Qf2+

7. Kg5–Qd2+

8. K×g4–Qe2+

9. K×h3–Qf1+

10. Kh4–(g)

10. ... –Q×d3

11. Rc7+– Mate.

(a) The Black K was able to move to b6 sq. That sq. is now under control of the N.

(b) To avoid attack by g3

(c) Prevents Black Q's return to h4

(d) Avoids exchange of Ps and tries for promotion.

(e) The Q could have taken h2 and then + K again. The Q now prevents Nb4+ by White, and can prevent queening of White's e-Pawn.

(f) Black can move only Q or b7.

(g) No move + is possible by the Q. Hence Black will play either Q×d3 or b6 only. In either case, White wins as above.

Two more solutions are possible by capturing Q and the other by queening c4 with the help of his K, but these are only academical.

GLOSSARY OF CHESS TERMS

Active	A piece is said to be active when it is well positioned.
Back now	The first rank of either side of the board.
Combination	When a series of moves are made, compelling the opponent to move in a particular way.
Development	Bringing the pieces to the square where they could be move active.
Diagonals	The standing rows of squares as shown in the first chapter.
Discovered Attack	A position in which one piece has been moved to uncover at attack by a Queen, Rook or Bishop.
Discovered Check	A position in which one piece has been moved to uncover check by another piece.
Double Check	A position in which a King is in check from two pieces at once.
Doubled Pawns	Pawns of the same colour standing on the same file.
En passant	A special kind of capturing move.
En prise	A piece is said to be 'en prise' when it is being attacked.
Escape square	A square to which an attacked piece may go to escape the attack.
Exchange	A series of moves in which each side captures pieces.
Exposed piece	The piece which is unable to find shelter.

Files	The vertical lines of squares on the board.
Flight square	An alternative term for escape square.
Forced move	A compulsory move.
Fork	A particular type of attack in which a piece threatens two enemy pieces simultaneously, like the Knight attacking the Queen and King simultaneously.
Gambit	An opening where a piece (usually a Pawn) is given up with the idea of gaining an advantage in development.
Guard	A piece which defends another, or a particular square, or provides protection.
Half Open File	A file on which there stands a Pawn (or Pawns) of only one colour.
Interpose	To move a piece in between an attacked piece and the attacker.
Isolated Pawn	One which has no Pawn of the same colour on either of the adjoining files.
J' adoube	"I adjust". Spoken by players when they wish to make clear that they are merely standing a piece correctly on its square, and not making a move.
Lines	Ranks, files or diagonals.
Major Piece	Queen or Rook.
Master	National Chess title awarded to selected players who have achieved a particularly high standard of chess in competitive play at an advanced level. The title of International Master is awarded by the International Chess

Federation (FIDE). The highest award in Chess, of Grandmaster, is also awarded by this body.

Minor Pieces Bishop or Knight.

Mobil Piece A piece which is able to move freely.

Open File A file on which there are no Pawns.

Opening File The set of first moves.

Overworked Piece A piece which is performing two or more deflusive roles at the same time.

Passed Pawn A Pawn which has no Pawn of the opponent in front of it, on its own file, and which in moving to the queening square does not have to pass an opponent's Pawn on either of the two adjoining file.

Perpetual Check A situation where check can be repeated non-stop.

Pin A piece is pinned when it cannot move without exposing another piece to attack.

Promotion When a Pawn is capable to reach the other end on the board and become a major piece, usually the Queen. When a Pawn becomes a Rook, Knight or Bishop, this is called under promotion.

Queening Promoting a Pawn to a Queen.

Ranks The horizontal squares which run left to right on the board.

Sacrifice Giving up a piece in order to gain some kind of advantage.

Simultaneous Display	An event in which one player plays a number of opponents at the same time, where the principal player makes a move on each board in turn.
Skewer	An attack upon two pieces on the same line, where the piece nearest the attacker is compelled to move, leaving other piece to be taken.
Smothered Mate	A checkmate by a Knight, where all the escape squares of the King are occupied by other pieces.
Stalemate	A drawn position where a player is not in check, but is unable to move any piece.
Tempo	Time taken to move pieces into required positions. A manoeuvre that need take only one move but is performed in two moves is said to lose a tempo. To force your opponent to make such time-wasting moves gains tempo for you.
Wing	The right or left-hand side of the board.
Winning the exchange	Gaining advantage in material as the result of an exchange of pieces. Generally this refers to capturing Rook or Knight or Bishop.
Zugszwang	A situation where the obligation to move is less an advantage than a handicap. It nearly always leads to loss of the game.

GOODWILL'S

PICK OF THE BEST CHESS PROBLEMS

COMPILED BY B.P. BARNES

These problems obey explicitly the rules of chess, and if you know the moves of the pieces, solving them will be well within your capabilities.That is not to say they are easy to solve -- they vary. The pleasure of problem chess lies not in the difficulty of solution, but in an appreciation of how White wins. There are no dull draws here, only exciting mate finishes !

The author, Barry Barnes, is an International Master and Judge of the F.I.D.E. for Chess Composition, its ex- 1st Vice President and Honorary Life Member. He edited the two-move problems in the specialist magazine *The Problemist* for 26 years.

Rs. 50

GOODWILL'S

FIRST MOVES

How to start a chess game

DAVID PRITCHARD

First Moves is an opening primer for the complete novice.
It offers clear, simple advice on how to start a
game of chess playing either as White or Black.
It is a book to be read, not studied.

When both sides are locked in combat it is easy to find plans.
But at the beginning, signposts are few.
Why move one man instead of another ?
First Moves will help you make the right decisions,
improve your game and get you thinking straight.

First Moves assumes no more than a knowledge of the rules of
chess. It ends where other opening books begin.

David Pritchard is the author of the standard beginner's chess
books *Right Way To Play Chess*
(which the Sunday Times described as "remarkable"), and
Begin Chess, whose combined sales in the
English language exceed half a million copies.

Rs. 45

GOODWILL'S

BASICS AND LAWS OF CHESS

B. K. CHATURVEDI

Basics and Laws of Chess

is meant for those learners

who wish to learn the game the easy way.

The basics and laws of the game

are explained in quite an elaborate style.

In order to make this book comprehensive

some chess problems have also been given

in a separate chapter.

Rs. 55

GOODWILL'S

WHITE TO PLAY AND MATE IN TWO

COMPILED BY B. P. BARNES

If you know the moves of the chess pieces - however well or badly you play - you will understand and enjoy these two-move chess problems. Each has a full solution and a lively commentary. You will be astonished at the depth and variety of the ideas shown, many of which you have never seen and never will see in over-the-board play.

The author, Barry Barnes, is an International Master and Judge of the F.I.D.E. for Chess Composition, its ex-1st Vice President and Honorary Life Member. He edited the two-move problems in the specialist magazine *The Problemist* for 26 years.

Rs. 55

GOODWILL'S

TECHNIQUES OF END-GAME IN CHESS

B.K. CHATURVEDI

Rs. 75

GOODWILL'S

TECHNIQUES OF MIDDLE-GAME IN CHESS

B.K. CHATURVEDI

Rs. 70